PRAISE FOR
GOD IS FOR REAL

"I've known Todd in times of success and challenge, in times of faith and fear. And in all those times, he's struck me as someone who sits at the feet of Jesus. In his prayers and his profession, he makes living Christian life real. GOD IS FOR REAL isn't just reflection, it's experience. And it inspires."

—Randall Wallace, director of the film *Heaven Is for Real*

"With GOD IS FOR REAL, Todd Burpo creates a powerful guide to life's FAQs about God, faith, and hope. Anyone who has lingering questions about God, his plan, and what it means for your life will find the answers you've been seeking in this book!"

—DeVon Franklin, *New York Times* bestselling author and producer of *Miracles from Heaven*

"In *Heaven Is for Real*, Todd Burpo shared his son's story about heaven and showed us what heaven is actually like. Now he gives us another masterpiece in his new book, GOD IS FOR REAL. In it, he answers the difficult questions about God, his role in our lives, why he allows bad things to happen, and so many more! This book is sure to help you gain a better understanding of how real God is in our everyday lives."

—Robert Morris, founding senior pastor of Gateway Church and bestselling author of *The Blessed Life*, *The God I Never Knew*, *Truly Free*, and *Frequency*

"Pain can feel like a prison...a dead end from which there is neither relief nor escape. GOD IS FOR REAL unveils its potential to open doors to crucial conversations about God and with God. Not simplistic answers, but the raw realities of hope in the midst of hurt."

—Wayne Schmidt, general superintendent of the Wesleyan Church and author of *Surrender*

"Here it is...tough questions that most people run around in their mind but are afraid to ask! The responses to these questions are not the typical pat answers. It is a powerful weave of personal experience, honest and authentic wrestling with the questions, and a fresh look at Scripture to find the answers. I found myself quickly turning the page to the next...it is compelling, thoughtful, new insight, and made me love God even more."

—Jo Anne Lyon, ambassador, general superintendent emerita of the Wesleyan Church and founder of World Hope International

"Pastor Todd Burpo does it again! I'll never forget my heart being ripped out as I read through the pages of *Heaven Is for Real*. Here we are again in GOD IS FOR REAL, discovering more practical truths about living with eternity in mind. Like many things God does in our lives we have an experience first and our understanding has to catch up. If *Heaven Is for Real* captured your heart like it did mine, GOD IS FOR REAL will equip you to learn why."

—Marcus Mecum, pastor of Seven Hills Church

GOD IS FOR REAL

AND HE LONGS TO ANSWER YOUR MOST DIFFICULT QUESTIONS

TODD BURPO

WITH **DAVID DRURY**

FaithWords

New York   Nashville

FaithWords
Hachette Book Group
1290 Avenue of the Americas, New York, NY 10104
faithwords.com
twitter.com/faithwords

First Edition: September 2017

FaithWords is a division of Hachette Book Group, Inc. The FaithWords name and logo are trademarks of Hachette Book Group, Inc.

The publisher is not responsible for websites (or their content) that are not owned by the publisher.

Scripture quotations marked (NLT) are taken from the Holy Bible, New Living Translation, copyright © 1996, 2004, 2007 by Tyndale House Foundation. Used by permission of Tyndale House Publishers, Inc., Carol Stream, Illinois 60188. All rights reserved.

Scripture quotations marked (NIV) are taken from the Holy Bible, New International Version®, NIV®. Copyright © 1973, 1978, 1984, 2011 by Biblica, Inc.™ Used by permission of Zondervan. All rights reserved worldwide. www.zondervan.com. The "NIV" and "New International Version" are trademarks registered in the United States Patent and Trademark Office by Biblica, Inc.™

Scripture quotations marked (ESV) are from The ESV® Bible (The Holy Bible, English Standard Version®). ESV® Permanent Text Edition® (2016). Copyright © 2001 by Crossway, a publishing ministry of Good News Publishers. The ESV® text has been reproduced in cooperation with and by permission of Good News Publishers. Unauthorized reproduction of this publication is prohibited. All rights reserved.

Scripture taken from the NEW AMERICAN STANDARD BIBLE®, Copyright © 1960, 1962, 1963, 1968, 1971, 1972, 1973, 1975, 1977, 1995 by The Lockman Foundation. Used by permission.

Library of Congress Control Number: 2017942513

ISBN: 978-1-4789-4812-4 (hardcover), 978-1-4789-4813-1 (ebook), 978-1-5460-3326-4 (international trade), 978-1-4789-2393-0 (large print)

Printed in the United States of America

LSC-H

10 9 8 7 6 5 4 3 2 1

CONTENTS

Contents

CONTENTS

I NEED A BIG GOD

My life is messy. Which God do I need to fix my mess?

I'm that small-town guy who is more comfortable getting my hands dirty working on a garage door than typing on this computer keyboard. I would also rather respond to an emergency pager or fire siren with my fellow firefighters than walk out on a stage to face a crowd of people.

When a family is crying together in pain or outrage at the hospital over the bed of a family member, I have a sense of belonging. It might be uncomfortable and painful, but something inside me says that I belong among the "dirty" situations—the traumas and struggles of life. It's not just the sense of being needed or useful that takes me to those places. It's also a sense of *understanding*. Pain is the humbling equalizer of humanity. Rich or poor, healthy or sick, we all eventually experience it. One way or another, all our hands get dirty.

So, I work with people and get dirty. Not just that, I *am* dirty! I live there amid the emotions, pain, and questions that everyone else struggles with, too. Life is hard, and the quick, clean, Disney World–style happily-ever-after solutions people throw around just downright offend me at times. This is especially true about the cheap, pat answers that come from some Christians. It's as if they live with a blind disconnect between this world and their "faith" world. I'd rather we all be *real* about these things.

My journey has been difficult. It's been crooked. Sometimes I feel like I'm moving in circles, not knowing how to get above life's challenges and see the meaning of it all!

And then *God.*

Yep, just *him.* God has a way of stepping into my mess and bringing me what I could never grab ahold of by myself.

I know that some of my life's story has been put on public display because of the book and movie *Heaven Is for Real.* Talk about awkward! I'm guessing that God is still laughing at me as I squirm even now just thinking about it. I do have to say that I am still amazed at actor Greg Kinnear's portrayal of me. I don't know how he observed me so quickly or if God gave him special help or both, but he showed my struggling fairly and downright realistically. The real Todd Burpo has issues—lots of them.

If you are like me, you have wondered out loud about the source of life's problems. I've been crushed personally at times, seeing people deal with hurts far greater than my own. Because of them, I live with a sense of gratitude that my problems aren't so bad in comparison.

So, what gives? Is it me? Or is it God? Or is it beyond me to even understand it all? But what do I do when God doesn't do what I thought he should have done?

When we were children, we all asked questions, *lots* of them. Being a parent reminds you of the awe of life as your little one starts asking for explanations and bounces with excitement at the next big thing life introduces to them. But now we are older, and life's just not as innocent as it once was. We keep problems to ourselves because our questions are now harder to answer, and the answers themselves are harder to grasp.

These days, though, I don't just find children asking me hard questions; I have met people around the world asking me about the broken parts of their lives and wondering out loud if God is big enough to deal with the dirt and hurt they are facing. Or is he too distant even to care about their problems in the first place? They just don't know. I understand their pain. I have asked those same questions myself.

I carry the heartache of burying a loved one. I have the scars of betrayal from people I trusted as friends. I have been lied about, mocked, and schemed against. Where is God in my yesterday, my today, and my tomorrow? Where is he in all of this dirt and mess?

One thing I've learned is to look for his presence in the pain. Instead of just trying to get an answer to make things make sense, I look for his presence in the stuff that doesn't make sense. If I look for him and am sensitive to it, I find him there in meaningful ways. Apparently, God gets his hands dirty just like I do.

Maybe that's why I feel I belong there in the dirt. God isn't afraid to be found there. I find him more ready and willing to respond to the broken and to the hard parts of people's lives than in the neatness and the "put-togetherness" of a nice and pretty church service.

Could it be that God is so big, our dirt doesn't bother him as much as it bothers us? Could it be that God isn't as put off by my failures and questions as I think he is? And could it be that he even gently laughs at me when I get mad?

I remember what I used to say to my children during their tantrums: "Are you done yet?" I would remind them that I was the parent and they weren't. Yes, I may have gotten angry with them at times. But not one of their fits ever threatened my love for them. It's just what the bigger person in a relationship does.

My friend John's life was changed when he brought this "bigger person" of God into his life. His struggle was alcohol. It consumed him.

After years of brokenness, I saw John in a grocery store one day, and he was excited. He announced that he had found Christ and that everything was different. John remembers what I said to him that day even though I forgot it myself. I believe it was one of those moments when God just took over.

John tells me I said, "Remember, you're *better off* now, but you're not *better than* anyone else."

Because that's where so many of us get put off when people talk to us about God, isn't it? There is that moment we sense them looking down their noses at us as they tell us about God. Then we step back from both that person and God rather than lean forward to think about what God could do in our own lives.

When people have this attitude, it doesn't sound like the Jesus we've heard about or would want to follow. When you try to ask for help with the problems you're going through, many of the people who seemed caring quickly become disinterested or even put off by the dirt and the mess.

Experiences like that can leave us with a bad taste in our mouths for spiritual things. That bad conversation or uncomfortable moment has the real danger of keeping us stuck in the past, resistant to God and to anyone else who might want to bring him up as a difference-maker in our lives.

God changed me from being chained to my low moments by using my son. Yes, I was and I still am a pastor. But I never have been all that put together. My life's issues had the ongoing tendency to rob my joy and weigh me down both emotionally and physically. You'll hear more about that in the pages to follow. But my son's confidence, innocence, simple childlike faith, and matter-of-factness about Heaven and the God who calls Heaven home astounded me. In fact, it just plain energized me.

The hope my son has for returning to Heaven is just as solid as his faith. He misses Heaven. He misses his sister, too. But he knows that he's going to see them both again one day. Truth be told, I have imagined meeting my daughter so many times now that I feel like I have had a chance to get to know her through my son. I miss her, too.

To this day, I still have a difficult time imagining how a God big enough to hold the world in his hands can exude so much love that a child stands in his presence completely unafraid. But that is exactly my son's description of God. The Bible even backs my son up. The writers in the Bible use more complicated words, but they still describe God the same way. I do believe that perfect love removes all fear, and my son has tried to describe that kind of big God love for years now.

My son is more than unafraid, however. He is drawn to the bigness of God. And why wouldn't he be? Who needs a small god? No one does. A small god is no good to anyone. But of course, there's a difference between *needing* and *wanting* what we need.

I *need* a big God, and so do you, but I didn't say I *want* a big God. Sometimes, I act as though I want a small god. I want a god that fits into my world. I want a neat and tidy god that fits on a chain around my neck, or on a bumper sticker on my truck. I want a god that does what I want him to do—one that fits my own personal philosophy.

Maybe I think a small god will be more convenient. I'd like my small god to be like the waiter of a restaurant, who brings my orders to the table fast and hot. If my coffee cup stayed full and if my every desire was not only met but anticipated, I would probably even tip my small god just a little bit more. And if there were an owner of the universal restaurant, I would be sure to note the areas that god could improve on before my next visit.

This "small god who serves me" attitude is a preposterous way to approach the real God, of course. But isn't that a bit of our instinct in the way we relate to God in this world?

Let's take a good long look at what God is *really* like. In our private moments on these pages, maybe you and I can look at one another with honesty and openness about the dirt in each of our lives and the questions we both ask about God. Big problems need big solutions—and our world creates some huge problems. Big questions need big answers—and a small god is not going to answer our questions. That small god will only cause more questions.

Let's talk about the things that scare us and challenge our

faith in God. Let's talk about the times we have been abandoned to despair and have struggled to hold on to hope. Let's talk about our search for true love and the hurts we need healing for. If we do that, I suspect at the end of this time together, both of us will have a bigger picture of God.

A small god could never help us have this talk. A small god wouldn't have it in him to face—let alone answer—these kinds of questions. But a big God might use this time to speak to both of us. That's just one of the reasons I need a big God, and so do you.

2

GETTING YOUR ATTENTION

Why should I even be interested in all this God-talk?

I was in Culver City, California, for some meetings, the part of Los Angeles where the Sony building is found. We were staying in a very old hotel called the Culver Hotel, one of those buildings shaped like a triangle because of two streets that separate at a sharp angle. I was tired and just wanted to get settled in our room for a good night's rest. A long drive that day followed by a long flight that evening had wiped me out.

This hotel had been restored to its old glory in the redesigned and refurbished rooms, but many things about its entrance were still a little odd. We walked into the ground floor with a bellhop who was on the street when we approached. The first floor of the hotel had no registration desk or anything—no lobby at all. Instead, it was a very crowded restaurant with a live band. The only thing my tired mind could pay attention to was the fact that the music was blaring. The familiar signage of most hotels was missing. If we hadn't had the bellhop guiding us through, we would have had no idea where to go. As the bellhop grabbed my wife's luggage, he agreed that the only way my wife and I were going to get much rest that night was if we lucked out and got a room on one of the top floors. He led us down a few odd corridors while we shimmied ourselves around those passing the other direction to a back elevator that took us up with our luggage to the floor above the band playing below.

On that next floor, I was expecting to find a normal hotel lobby (thinking perhaps we had just entered the wrong side of the building), but instead, the clunky elevator doors opened to a long hallway of various-size hotel conversation rooms, probably designed for business travelers or occasional family reunions. There was a small desk in the hallway like you'd find in a dorm room. A lady was sitting behind it. The bellhop led us there, and the lady at the desk began to ask the standard registration questions. I was a bit out of sorts at this point. I didn't realize that going to the town where they make surreal movies would feel so much like I was living in a surreal movie myself.

As I gave my information, I realized that the thumping bass from the band downstairs was reverberating the floor beneath my feet, and I could even make out the words of the songs. I continued to worry if I would get the rest I needed that night. One look in my wife's eyes and I could tell she was thinking the same thing. I had asked the bellhop earlier how late the band would be playing and he told me it could be 1 or 2 a.m.

I thought back to the street view of this oddly shaped triangular hotel and remembered that it went several stories up, perhaps even six stories or more. As we were being registered, I sighed a bit, in a sort of audible representation of the simple, selfish, but necessary prayer in my heart at that moment: *Please, God, I need to sleep!*

The bellhop helped us gather our things, and we entered the elevator again. Without even having to ask, the lady at the desk had graciously assigned us a room located on the second-highest floor of the hotel. As we traveled slowly up the elevator shaft, I could hear the music receding into the distance. My shoulders relaxed as I started thinking of the sleep I would get in just a few short moments once we unloaded. I also had an undeniable feeling of gratefulness knowing that God had just responded to my simple but desperate prayer.

FORCE OR FAVOR

Throughout the historic hotel there were many pictures from *The Wizard of Oz*, particularly those featuring the actors who played the Munchkins in the film. Apparently, all the Munchkins from *The Wizard of Oz* stayed in this very hotel when it was filmed. When I told this part of the story to people back home in Nebraska, they had some good fun with me, because I'm such a short guy: "You should have felt right at home in the Munchkin Hotel, Todd!" My basketball friends know just how to rub it in!

Fortunately, as we exited the elevator on our floor, I could feel that great wave of sleep expectation flow over me as I no longer heard the sound of the band below. You know how you feel just a few minutes before sleeping after a long, hard day of work or travel? That was me. I hadn't paid a great deal of attention to the bellhop until then, but as he carried our things out of the elevator, he said to me, "Wow, the Force must be with you!"

I looked at him a little blankly, not understanding, since I was already practically snoring where I stood. He explained, "You must have used the Force to get this room up here on this floor, because you got exactly what you wanted—most don't." I'm sure you can imagine my wife Sonja's eyes rolling. She knew his comment bothered me and just wanted me to let it pass, but...I couldn't ignore it.

I shook my head and just said flatly, "Well, actually the Force has nothing to do with it. I'm not a Jedi, son. I don't much believe in karma, either. Instead, I prayed that I would get a good night's sleep, and God provided. That wasn't the *Force*, that was God's *favor*." I said this not thinking much of it. I wasn't trying to have a deeply spiritual conversation with this bellhop, but I couldn't let his "Force" comment go without just a little bit of truth slipping out of my mouth.

As we unloaded into the room, the bellhop did something I've seen many times before when I bring up God to people: He changed the subject to some other benign story that related to God, but only to end the conversation. My talk of praying for a good night's sleep and getting my prayer answered must have made him uncomfortable.

He stuttered his way through the first part of the sentence, but eventually said, "Yeah, there's this kid who went to Heaven and they wrote a book and they're going to make a movie about it or something."

I looked over at my wife and she gave me another look, knowing this would start a much longer conversation than she had intended for us to have with our bellhop. But even she nodded slightly and agreed that God was calling me out. As I held out the tip for him I said, "That's me. That's my son you're talking about. That's why we're here."

I've never seen a bellhop ignore a tip before. His mouth opened so wide I could see his tonsils as he stared back at me. I saw realization wash over him in that long pause. I mean, what were the odds? Out of the billions of people on Planet Earth, the parents of the little boy from the book and coming movie were the very ones he was facing. His attempt to dodge a conversation about God had backfired.

I filled the awkward silence of the moment by saying, "I think God's trying to get your attention. Do you know he cares about you just as much as me or my son?" By the look in his eyes, I could tell that this small-framed eighteen-year-old who was hustling for tips had realized a new truth for what might have been the first time in his short life. He mattered to God. Movies may refer to "the Force" at work in space dramas on the big screen, but moments like this undeniably point us to the real God.

How is God trying to get your attention? As you read this book right now, think about what is happening in your life, and how God might be orchestrating events to get your attention. He's a big God, and he works in big ways.

How many God moments have you had to explain away? Have you walked away from a wreck that you shouldn't have? I did. Have you survived an emergency surgery or a cancer scare? I have. Have you had a stranger's generosity, a song or message on the radio, or a conversation with a friend occur at crucial moments in your life's journey, as if they were being orchestrated by someone bigger than you and the others in your world? You bet, all that's happened to me, too.

One of the men who eventually produced the *Heaven Is for Real* movie said this to me: "I can't sleep at night. God won't let me. I have to make this movie about what your son saw." Now, he didn't give me any more details than that, but in some way he had come to the conclusion that he couldn't deny that God was the one interrupting his life.

But we are just beginning our discussion together. We will go on to talk about hard questions, deep mysteries, and problems great and small and annoying. All of these matters are often brought up as doubts, possible reasons why we don't trust God, or why we maybe shouldn't believe in God or listen to those who do. I'm guessing you have many of these questions already rolling around in your heart and mind. I hope to offer helpful wisdom on these things, I really do.

But I believe that something more, something bigger, is happening as you read this right now. These questions you have, the pain you face, the struggles you see in the world today: These are all things God is using to get your attention. He isn't fazed by your questions—he wants you to ask them, especially your most difficult questions. And he doesn't mind staying in the hard parts with you. I don't mind, either.

My job is not to do public relations for God. Instead, we'll face the hard stuff and see if we can find God in the middle of it all. It won't be a made-up God who solves everything for you like a genie in a lamp. It will be the real God who exists even in the hard and dirty parts of life.

If God is trying to get your attention, I hope you'll give it to him.

3

NEW LIFE IN NEWTOWN

*Can I do something about the dark and ugly evil that exists
in this world, even in me?*

What were you doing the morning of December 14, 2012? It was a regular day in my hometown in Nebraska; I bet you'd call it boring. I got the kids off to school and headed out to work. With Christmas only eleven days away, most in my town were pleasantly distracted by school programs, special services at the church, and the presents we would buy to put around the tree.

Then halfway through the morning we heard the news of a shooter in a small town on the East Coast.

Ten times more people live in Newtown, Connecticut, than my town of Imperial, Nebraska, but it is a pretty small town by comparison on the East Coast. With a population of about twenty-seven thousand, Newtown has been there for three hundred years, sitting sixty miles outside of New York City, where some nine million people live. Still, Newtown is a quiet place, with only one homicide in a decade. Until December 14, 2012.

The shooter entered Sandy Hook Elementary School and began to fire. First he killed the principal and school psychologist in the hallway, and then he walked into a classroom of first graders. There, a tragic sequence of events took place. The substitute teacher had wisely pushed the children toward a bathroom. But the shooter found them and killed all but one little girl.

That brave little girl hid there, staying very still among her friends, playing dead and somehow not getting hit, and later she sneaked out of the room.

In less than ten minutes, 152 bullets were fired, and twenty children and six adults were dead. A teacher from another school in town said what I might have said about my town, and perhaps you about yours: "Stuff like this does not happen in Newtown."

But it did.

Why?

Not long after the shootings, I started to get requests for us to send our book to Newtown for people dealing with the tragedy. These requests mostly came from those who had been touched by the story, and they thought it might help. We didn't get involved in this way, as even a well-intentioned effort to help can hurt those in the middle of such a tragedy. So, we kept our distance and just prayed.

I personally could scarcely wrap my mind around this event. My youngest child, Colby, was about the same age as those in that first-grade classroom, although he was in second grade at the time. If this happened in our town, I wouldn't even know what to say. I think it's normal to admit that. It's okay not to know what to say. But I do know where to turn, and that's to God.

Along with the rest of the country, as I grappled with this horrible event, I started to ask questions. My questions all started with "Why?"

WHY DIDN'T WE KNOW ABOUT THIS MADMAN?

I wanted to know why we didn't have this guy on a list somewhere. Why didn't we see this monster a mile away? Of course, no one saw him as a monster until that moment. They saw him as a relative, a neighbor, a student, even a son. It turns out that the shooter was a seemingly quiet young man with no criminal record. But he still killed his mother in their home before driving to nearby Sandy Hook. He was a bit of a recluse, and had his challenges, but nobody who knew him or treated him saw this coming. It was a mass shooting with no clear motive. There is no helpful answer to this "Why." So, we have more questions...

WHY WASN'T THE SCHOOL MORE SECURE?

No one expected the level of violence that day, but some precautions were already taken there. The school had gone through lockdown drills just a few weeks earlier. The safety policy meant that you had to ring a doorbell at the front after the doors locked that morning. But that didn't stop the shooter, who shot through a large panel of glass adjacent to the door to gain entrance. Many schools instituted new policies after Newtown, but most of those were merely safety policies that Sandy

Hook already had in place at the time of the shooting. There is no helpful answer to this "Why," either. So, we keep asking questions...

WHY WASN'T IT STOPPED BY POLICE OR STAFF?

Small-town first responders, like those in Newtown, know what the buildings are like, and they often know the people in those buildings. I'm a first responder myself, and on the way to a fire a whole list of pre-planning questions go through my mind: Which way is the wind blowing? What weather changes are coming? But for Sandy Hook, there is no way to pre-plan. There is no training that prepares you for that. There is no fire truck that can put out the immensity of this dark burn in such a lost human heart.

Multiple stories of heroism came out soon after the tragedy. The six adults killed all lost their lives by confronting the shooter while trying to protect kids. Teachers helped kids out of windows or ushered them to closets and bathrooms to hide. The first officers were on the scene in fewer than five minutes from the very first 911 call, after which the shooter promptly shot himself even before the officers entered the building. This "Why" leads nowhere, so we keep asking...

WHY DID HE HAVE ALL THOSE GUNS?

Officials investigating the incident noted that the guns weren't the shooter's in the first place. They were his mother's guns, which he took from her and then used to kill her, followed by those at Sandy Hook. In retrospect, we all think he shouldn't have had access to his mother's guns, but again nobody saw it coming. Unable to find answers for this one situation, we ask bigger questions...

WHY DOES THIS HAPPEN SO OFTEN?

Newtown doesn't want to be known for and defined by this tragedy, but it joined the list of other places where horrible killings occurred: San Bernardino, Charleston, Chattanooga, Fort Hood, the Washington Navy Yard, Aurora, and Columbine. In the United States, we are deeply concerned that this happens so very often. These are added to the list of towns and cities around the world where mass killings have also taken place, like Sang-Namdo, Hungerford, Kunming, Cuers, Port Arthur, Sagamihara, Erfurt, Akihabara, and Utøya. What is happening in the world? Are there *really* that many of us who are ready to snap and kill people? We can't seem to answer this question. So, I wonder if we need to ask a bigger "Why?"

THE BIG WHY

All these questions are legitimate, and we need to keep asking them. Sometimes there are answers. Sometimes there's something we *can* do. But often we just need to admit that the world is filled with *evil*. Ordinary people can have the capacity to do unbelievable evil. In many, if not most, of these cases we hear about, those who knew the killer say that before the tragedy the person seemed "normal" even if a little odd. Usually nobody sees it coming.

When I think about the shooting in Sandy Hook, and picture that shooter heading into a room of first graders and doing this, I am gripped by the darkness of it all. I don't care how many lights were on in that schoolroom. As he walked in there with his finger on the trigger, a darkness spread into that place that is bigger and more complex and more abysslike than can be contained in any one person. It is Darkness with a capital *D*.

This darkness is the big "Why."

How could someone do this? To children?

ADJUSTING TO THE DARK

This is what happens to us when these events take place: We get used to the darkness around us because it is gradual. But these tragedies show us just how dark we are, as humans, inside. Have you noticed how your eyes adjust to the dark? When the lights go out abruptly, you can barely tell where the walls are. But then if you wait a bit, your eyes adjust and you get comfortable again.

The same thing happens in our world. Darkness creeps into life much the way the sun sets in the evening: gradually. And we adjust to the absence of light just as our lives also adjust to the absence of God. I know people who used to pray. But they eventually got busy and distracted. Slowly, the God they heard about as a child was replaced by entertainment promoting violence. The manners and dignity they displayed at one time were replaced with the name-calling and vulgarity of comedy and politics. They don't have time to read about God or visit a church, but they fill their hours watching the news reports about wars and victims of crime. Terrorism and bombings have become common, and family prayers and values have become scarce. People have become accustomed to the dark and the evil possibilities that accompany it.

So often, as with this tragedy in Newtown, we find that no one saw it coming in the perpetrator. Nobody could have guessed that this man would be the one to cause such pain. He probably never would have guessed it, either. My guess is that he adjusted to the idea of his evil acts gradually. Either through hurts inflicted on him by others or by failed dreams that he might have blamed on God, the man gradually became capable of lashing out with violence. He couldn't see the evil growing in his life before it was too late for those innocent children and teachers. Somehow the light from goodness and God became so dim that no alarms were sounding in his life to wake him up.

We might come up with all kinds of people and things and systems to blame, but it is clear that at least one thing is common among them all: evil.

Why are we so vulnerable to evil? Why don't we have any protection?

Our big "Why" needs a big *God* to answer it. In the end, I ask these questions not to my family members, not to the news reporters, not even to my church. I ask these questions to God directly. Only God can respond to questions like this and make a difference. Newtown seemed to be one of those places where only a special light could break through such deep darkness.

I talked of when the lights go out, but have you ever been in a dark place when suddenly the lights went *on*? It is shocking.

It makes you close your eyes and maybe even hold a hand up, shielding against the light. Light penetrates darkness and interrupts our comfort zone since our eyes have adjusted to the dark.

What if you wait just long enough for your eyes to adjust to the light? Could spiritual light do to evil what physical light does to darkness? Could fear be replaced by peace and security? Could our wandering be replaced with a clear sense of direction? Could light lead us to the ones we love and out of the lonely dark?

TEXAS

A few months after the Sandy Hook shooting, I found myself in Texas in a very nice dining room at a steak house. Everyone was dressed up for the special function with tablecloths and fine china. It was fancy, but it was also Texan, meaning everything was big and bold.

At this dinner, a woman came up to me who was in her thirties, and fairly short (and by that, I mean she was still a little bit taller than me). She had two super-cute little girls with her, a two-year-old and a four-year-old.

This woman said, "Thank you for sharing your story." I asked why she said that. She began to cry and shared that her daughter had died in the Sandy Hook shooting. As she unloaded her heart, I started to cry. I remember her daughter's name, which I won't mention here, but to lose the treasure of that little girl is unimaginable.

She told me that after the shooting she had more than thirty copies of the *Heaven Is for Real* book given to her. I was embarrassed and so I just said, "I'm sorry." She said, "No, I really couldn't believe that one book had impacted so many people I know. But I'm not thanking you for that—I want to thank you for the *Heaven Is for Real for Kids* because it's the best way we've found to talk about all this with these girls. We read it every night." As our conversation went on, these little girls started to quote our book back to us. I realized that for this family, the book was a resource helping them explain death and the afterlife to two little girls who missed their sister. Instead of just tears, they now talked about what their sister was doing in Heaven every day. This tragedy was not the end. Smiles and laughter returned in some moments. Light was starting to shine.

HEAVEN'S LIGHT

Not long after that time in Texas, we found ourselves officially invited to one of the largest churches in the Newtown area. Of course, I think all the churches in Connecticut could fit inside some of the churches I've seen in Texas. But still, it could seat a lot of people.

As I prepared to speak, I was confronted by my lack of words for this mother I had met in Texas. I remember thinking, *These are hurting people struggling with such huge darkness, and I'm just a wrestling coach who preaches on the weekend. Are you sending the right guy, God?*

We felt led to go there with a message from the first chapter of the book of John: "The light shines in the darkness, and the darkness can never extinguish it."[1] We believed that no matter how deep that darkness in Sandy Hook was, that light couldn't be destroyed by it—even there.

That night my son Colton had just turned fourteen years old, and he sang for the first time a song called "Heaven" based on Colton's own words as written in *Heaven Is for Real for Kids*. It was such a special moment. As he sang, the tone of the gathering went from somber mourning to cheering joy. I sat stunned, sitting in the front row next to a Newtown policeman who was working security for the event.

As Colton came out to sing later on in this event, two little girls rushed up the platform steps to shake his hand on stage, right in front of everyone. As they went back to their seats I noticed the policeman crying, his tears reaching all the way down his neck to his collar.

I leaned over to this man and asked if I could do anything. He shook his head and told me he was just overwhelmed because he knew one of those two little girls. He repeated to himself, "That's her. That's her."

Now I was really confused. "I don't know who you are talking about. What do you mean by *her*?" I asked.

"I didn't know she was here. I didn't notice her or her family come in the room tonight, but that's the little girl who survived the shooting in the first-grade classroom," he cried.

That's when I started to cry, too. The light can shine through even the deepest darkness. How could a little girl who had experienced something so evil feel safe enough to rush the stage and shake my son's hand in front of such a large crowd of people?

I was seized with the reality that God does do something about evil. This was a defining moment for me: I realized that no matter what anyone else says, we can pierce through the darkness, and it is worth it to bring the light of God to those deeply hurt by the darkness in this world. Regardless of how inadequate I feel about myself, I will never forget the chance that God gave to us to encourage that very special little girl. I felt like God was saying that day, "Don't you dare turn off your light."

4

NOT PERFECT, JUST DEVOTED

What does God really want from me?

These days it is very difficult for most volunteer fire department ments across the country to be fully staffed. The growing demands of training don't sit well with most people I know. Working hours upon hours without pay takes its toll. And with the firefighter usually working a full-time job somewhere else, family time usually takes a serious hit. Most employers aren't helpful, either. Paying employees to leave work or simply allowing them to leave work to fight fires is not very profitable for businesses.

Despite these challenges, our fire department in Imperial is one of the most respected volunteer departments across the state of Nebraska. We've earned a reputation for being professional and well trained. Our department is one of the very few that manages to keep a full roster with a waiting list of candidates looking to join. I am very proud to be a part of that team.

I don't know all the reasons why this high level of performance and commitment to our friends and neighbors remains, but I do know one reason. At each meeting we hold, our volunteers recite "The Fireman's Creed." It goes like this:

"We hereby pledge to willingly give our services as firemen, to those persons in need in any emergency, be it civil or local, in order to preserve to the best of our ability, life and property. We hereby accept the hazards imposed in order that we may best serve this cause!"

Much like a soldier's pledge to the flag, this has been our pledge to our community and to each other before we begin every meeting. It reminds us to stay focused on our mission! Why? The reason is that causes like saving lives are worthy of our devotion, even if that devotion requires taking risks and making sacrifices.

JOINING UP

According to my mom, I always wanted to be a firefighter when I was a young boy. So I guess my acting on the desire that God put in me at a young age was inevitable. However, when I decided to actually take the risk and become a fireman, it was an awkward step for me.

When I first asked about joining the fire department in Imperial, I had a lot of questions about what I would be doing as a firefighter. I also had a lot of questions about what training would be required. Those thoughts even caused me to wonder if I had the stuff it would take to become a good firefighter. What's the point of joining in the first place if I wouldn't be able to measure up later?

I think many people have these same reservations about joining up with God. Maybe something is drawing you out to seek God, but you aren't sure about wanting the God you find. He has gotten your attention, but maybe you're concerned about having the stuff it takes to belong to God.

Perhaps you have hard questions about God.

"What does God expect out of me? I have heard so many different things about God. I wouldn't have a clue what God would really want from me."

"I let myself down all the time. If I don't measure up to my own standards or commitments, how could I measure up to God's expectations? If I seek God, am I starting a journey that I honestly just can't finish or live up to?"

"Do I risk being rejected? Maybe I'm just not good enough to even be considered. Like tryouts in front of a coach in sports, are there tryouts in front of God?"

Many people don't know where to take these questions and doubts to find answers. I have found Jesus Christ the best place to find answers to questions pertaining to God.

When someone wants to find the truth about God, Jesus lovingly connects and points them in the right direction. He is also unafraid to tell us about what might be getting in our way to God. He sometimes answers questions that we didn't even think of asking.

EVERLASTING QUESTION

Heaven has been on the hearts of all generations. What happens when we die? And isn't life better somewhere else? After all this struggle, after all these relationships, and after all our experiences, we seem to have this sense that we don't just get deleted at death like some computer program. Something about a human has everlasting value.

One such honest individual brought his thoughts and his questions to Jesus. Like the rest of us, he had a pretty good idea of what he wanted from God.

Of course, this man had heard from others and had read from Scriptures things about God. He even had an accurate sense of some of the things God would like in his life. But did he really understand what God wanted most from him?

So this man that the Bible described as a rich, young ruler ran over to Jesus and knelt in dramatic fashion, paying him a compliment. "Good teacher" he began. He then asked his question: "What must I do to inherit everlasting life?"

Jesus responded in the straightforward way any first-century rabbi would: "But to answer your question, you know the commandments."[1] Jesus knew that the young man knew these commandments, but he listed off a few as examples: "You must not murder. You must not commit adultery. You must not steal. You must not testify falsely. You must not cheat anyone. Honor your father and mother."

The rich young ruler got an answer he could certainly live with, because he had followed every one of the commandments since he was a small boy. He told Jesus this.

But Jesus wasn't done. Others might have been. But Jesus knew more about this man. Jesus knew there was something that gripped his heart and controlled his decisions. And Jesus was not going to let this go. Why? Because of love.

Mark 10:21 said it this way: "Looking at the man, Jesus felt genuine love for him."

It's important to remember this when we read what Jesus said next. When Jesus tells us, "There is still one thing you haven't done," it isn't because he is trying to be difficult, or that we have some bar to jump over to prove our worth to him. It isn't even because that "one thing" is the thing other people need to do, too. He tells us these things because he *loves* us and he sees what is keeping us from giving to God the one thing God wants most. For the rich young ruler, his wealth held him back from a full devotion to God, his eyes always on his treasure because possessions were the main thing for him in life.

Jesus said, "Go and sell all your possessions and give the money to the poor, and you will have treasure in heaven. Then come, follow me."

The rich young ruler's smile dropped. His shoulders slumped. His head hung. He walked away.

YEAR SEVEN

The number seven is a lucky number for many. But for marriage statistics, year seven is often a frightful number. Many divorces happen at year seven.

My year seven was at risk of that. Yes, I'm a pastor, yes, I love God, and yes, I love my wife, but I still almost lost my marriage at year seven.

"I don't know if I love you anymore." That was the hardest and most painful sentence I have ever heard Sonja say to me.

The blow wounded me deeper than any blow I have ever taken. I hurt so much I couldn't find enough air to breathe evenly.

When we both said, "Until death do us part," I know that we both meant it. But what had happened to us in seven years? Sonja was ready to leave, and I needed to figure things out fast.

For starters, we had moved. Sonja had to give up many of her friends when we moved to pastor a small, no...a *tiny* church in Imperial. We had almost no income from the church, so I was working all the extra hours I could to establish my business.

I was preaching and visiting the few members of my congregation. If anyone called, I answered. I didn't want to disappoint anyone in my first solo pastorate. I was also trying to be the best dad I could be to our irresistible little one-year-old daughter, Cassie.

I hadn't lost Sonja yet, but somewhere I had lost my *devotion to* her. I was busy, but she was home alone with Cassie, idle and very much forgotten.

Now, Cassie—well, she had nothing to complain about. All day Sonja would read to her, play with her, sleep when she could, and feed her. When Dad got home, I would play and laugh and show Cassie how important she was while my wife watched the two of us wrestle on the floor.

Before Cassie came along and before we moved, we were "Dinks." "Dual Incomes No Kids." We had both the time and the money to just give to each other automatically, I guess. It was easy to be in love. So I can't say that I ever had to make a hard decision to live in a devoted way with Sonja. It wasn't hard.

Right after Sonja announced that she was ready to leave, I begged her to give me a weekend for the two of us to take a vacation and figure things out. She agreed. Of course then we found out that my dad's father had passed away, and the funeral was scheduled at the same time as that last-chance vacation. I was the only grandchild who failed to make it to Grandpa's funeral. Despite the angst from my family, I was just starting to learn how to become a truly devoted husband and make those sacrifices.

We talked for hours about what had happened to us. Then we both decided that some changes were worth trying. Next to God, the best thing we could give to our daughter was a good marriage. But we had work to do.

We started to put Cassie to bed earlier. She was no longer allowed in our bed, either. Date night was also established. Babysitters were hired.

Cassie fussed a bit, but you might have guessed it. She survived.

Every day Sonja and I took time to talk to each other. Even if it was just ten minutes, it happened. What had come naturally before Cassie was now becoming intentional and regular.

I also started to care more about what Sonja thought about me than what my few church people did or the customers of my fledgling business.

The more devotion I gave, the more Sonja realized she had my heart again. Instead of running after other people's approval, I was pursuing her again. The forgotten one was now valued.

Then gradually, it happened. Sonja decided she loved me again. All it took was devotion.

NATURAL

We just celebrated our twenty-sixth wedding anniversary. I continue to be amazed at what Sonja can put up with from me today. If you were to ask her about her husband, though, she could still tell you about the dozens if not hundreds of flaws I have.

For starters, I'm not the best help around the house. I refuse to ever attend another ballet with her. And I do make fun of all the shoes she buys. And this list is just the beginning. I've put on a few pounds. I've picked up pig hunting with a passion. And my allergies and coughing make it hard for her to get a good night's sleep anymore.

But today, I am completely devoted to her. There are safeguards all over my life to prevent even a hint of interest in another woman. I take lunch to her at her school. I enjoy surprising her with the occasional flowers, and we also go on walks together because she hates "my" workouts.

Even though my flaws have to be managed, they never seem to challenge her love for me. Why? Because Sonja knows today that I am devoted to her. And that devotion *makes* our marriage. I know I would never score a hundred on any marriage test, but Sonja knows that I am completely hers, 100 percent. My kids know it, too. Just a couple of weeks ago, Colton shared with both of us that he wanted to have a marriage just like ours.

I know that some people today don't believe devotion in marriage is possible because they have only found that passion, or convenience, or lust, or money, or status, or some other short-lived emotion have sustained it this far. Like wealth for the rich young ruler, they have a history of trying to be in a relationship with somebody while loving something else. But their actions betray them. Many continue to remarry, hoping that the next person will give them the devotion they are still longing to find. They want to get devotion, but they struggle to give it.

God has the same desire for you. You might think you have to be successful to please God, just as you do to please some people. You might assume that God wants you to make some tremendous sacrifices in order to keep him happy. Surely, pleasing God has to be hard, right? Well, now that I am devoted to Sonja, pleasing her has actually become pretty natural. When you love someone, showing love isn't hard. Sure, you still experience hard things together, but loving someone you're devoted to is fulfilling and rewarding. In many cases our devotion to one another helps us get through the hard times.

JUST DEVOTED

There is a huge difference between *perfect* and *devoted*. God knows the difference. We know the difference. But be honest: Isn't *devotion* what you really want someone to give to you when he or she says, "Forsaking all others, until death do us part"?

I bet you've seen couples who have remained in love and have proven that devotion is doable, even in a flawed earthly relationship. Couldn't devotion be even more possible if a righteous, compassionate, and generous God was in that relationship?

If we want special people in our lives to be devoted to us, couldn't we agree with God? He has the right to look for devotion from us. If we can accept a few flaws from the people who love us, could God also work with our flaws as long as we still love him?

THREE TIMES

Scriptures describe God as compassionate, slow to anger, and abounding in love to those who seek him. And Jesus demonstrated all of these qualities to a man named Peter.

Peter is one of my favorite people to read about in the stories of Jesus. He was bold yet dangerous. When he spoke, his friends just never knew if he was going to say something profound or embarrassing. He was hardworking but unable to stay awake for some of the prayers that Jesus had asked him to pray. He stood up to a mob with just one sword and then froze in fear beside a fire, with a young girl asking him about his relationship to Jesus.

Jesus had given Peter his name. His parents had called him Simon. But God saw someone who would become a rock and a leader among the rest of Jesus' followers. The name Peter means "rock." But Peter started off kind of flaky; the man named for rock seemed a lot more like shale than granite.

You would think that God would just give up and try again with someone else after a while. But Jesus didn't treat Peter that way. Jesus knew Peter wasn't perfect. And after Peter had managed to deny Jesus three times in one night, Jesus didn't remind Peter of his mistakes; he reminded him of what mattered most.

Jesus already knew Peter was hurting. He didn't need to manage Peter's flaws, either. Jesus just needed to let Peter know that love and forgiveness can lead to growth and restoration.

Jesus asked him one simple question a number of times. "Peter, do you love me?" If so, "then feed my sheep."

If you're still devoted, let's move forward, Peter. I'm not finished with you. I still love you. You still belong to me. That's what Jesus does for the devoted.

BLOOPER AWARDS

If I said being a firefighter is all work and no play, I would be lying. The rush of adrenaline, the sound of sirens, the big trucks, and the thrill of attacking a fire are among the upsides. Not too many desk jobs leave you with a story at the end of the day. Fighting fires gives you all kinds of things to talk about, and for others to talk about.

My department relishes the opportunity to hand out the annual bloopers award at the end of each year. It might not be the most distinguished of awards, but it is the one that everyone talks about the most. A firefighter might even pray about it: *Oh God, please let someone else get the blooper award this year!*

It was a typical Nebraska summer afternoon when the alarm went off. We had just seen a new hotel built and open for business in Imperial, and it was a bit surprising that such a new building would be sounding its alarm. Without hesitation, I jumped in my POV—personal operating vehicle (which is a fancy name for my pickup)—and drove to the fire station. When I arrived, our rescue truck was filling up and preparing to leave. Being one of the men authorized to wear an air pack, I jumped in our truck and claimed the last available seat. From this point, things went downhill for me.

You see, that day had not been a normal one. Earlier in the morning I had returned from a nearby hospital. I had suffered a kidney stone attack the week before, and doctors concluded that I needed a lithotripsy surgery. My stone had measured six millimeters from the tests conducted while I was in the ER. It was something far too large to pass without being blasted into smaller pieces.

That morning, they had put me to sleep and given me electrical zaps like I was Frankenstein. With one pad in front of my left kidney and another behind it, the doctor shot electricity back and forth like a tennis ball between two rackets until the kidney stone inside was pulverized into smaller but passable pieces. It was a strange experience, because when I woke up from this procedure there was not a mark on me. The urologist who debriefed me said I would be fine and released me to go home. I'm pretty sure I heard him say, "You shouldn't have any problems." Even though my wife was there to drive me home, I guess I forgot to ask how long it would take before the drugs that they had given me in surgery would wear off.

Once our fire trucks arrived at the hotel, I jumped out and tried to put on my gear, but I couldn't find the knob to turn my air bottle on, not to mention the hose that attaches the bottle to my mask. Fortunately, a quick all-clear was given. It was just a false alarm. Sometimes new alarm systems have to get the bugs worked out. But then the chief came over, called me aside, and asked me a question that I'm sure he's still laughing about today. It's also one he probably never thought he would ever ask his pastor, either: "Um, Todd, are you *on* something?" I was standing there confused, with my pack upside down. Obviously, I must have looked kind of ridiculous.

That's when I realized the answer was an embarrassing, "Uh, yes." The medication I'd been given for the procedure was still affecting me, and I hadn't even thought of it when I responded to the call. Our fire department has a policy that nobody can respond while under the influence—which I've always thought was a great policy. Of course, I never thought *I* would be the one breaking it.

It would have been at minimum silly and perhaps even stupid for me to not admit the problem to my fire chief and tell him he was right. He was pointing out an issue everyone could see but me. I was drugged up and in no condition to be on a fire scene that day.

Fortunately, someone else left his POV in drive instead of park that year when responding to a fire. After it slowly rolled over the curb and stopped in the side of the lawyer's office across the street, he won the blooper award and my prayers were answered.

After enjoying another sixteen years of fighting fires, these guys have seen my commitment to them and to the fire service. They have looked past my stupidity and have given me the grace to keep serving alongside them.

Part of why I like Peter the rock must be because I have so much in common with him. I'm not perfect, just devoted.

5

HIDE (BLAME) AND SEEK

Complete honesty is hard for me. Can God handle the thoughts I hide from everyone else?

It is hard to hide things from my wife. My kids know this, because she's "all up in their business," as they say. She knows their passwords, knows who they are texting, and knows what videos they are watching. They call her stalker-Mom. She doesn't care. We figure it's our job as parents to know this stuff (but of course, it's Mom who knows this stuff, because I'm clueless). Which is also why she knows all about me. She's got all my passwords, too—and knows the same stuff about me.

It goes far beyond technology. Sometimes I'll get up in the night when I can't sleep. Without supervision in the middle of the night, from time to time, yes, I will admit it, I do some snacking. Once she asked me about the honey buns I ate. I remember wondering how in the world she knew about those— I'd thrown away the wrapper! But I had to admit it—yes, I ate them when I thought she was unaware and sound asleep. Apparently even sleep doesn't affect her ability to know things.

This is all a real problem when we have a very good reason to keep something from her. One of her love languages is receiving and giving gifts, so surprising her with gifts matters a lot, and I've learned that I cannot hide those from her in the house. I should say "her house," because even though I sleep there and have a few drawers to call my own, it's her house, really, and everyone knows it. So, I've resorted to keeping gifts in my truck for weeks at a time to hide them from her, which is not very convenient. But I have to, because if it enters the house, she somehow knows about it. The CIA or the KGB could learn a few things from my wife.

My wife is practically omniscient (all-knowing). But of course, she's *not* omniscient *really*. That word, *omniscient*, is one we use to describe God, because only God can truly know all things. I can hide a few things from my wife still, even beyond gifts in my truck.

For instance, I can hide all kinds of things from my wife that I am *thinking* about. She doesn't know what my thought life is unless I tell her. And even when I tell her about it, I don't tell her *all* about it, with all the gory details. She could even have cameras on me right now, but not know what I'm thinking. I can hide things from her. I don't want to, but I sure can. Our relationship will always have that barrier; there will always be that challenge to intimacy. A marriage is a lot about managing that challenge, and still being one with each other.

With God, there is no barrier like I have with my wife and with every other relationship in the world. There is no challenge for God when it comes to knowledge. He knows exactly what I'm thinking. God knows my thoughts in every specific detail. So, there is no barrier that I could build that God can't see through. But I still try to build the same ones with him that have worked so well with other people. Don't you?

He knows your thoughts as well. But people only see our true attitudes and problems when we act out or say things that should have been filtered first. I have a friend who keeps this sign on the counter of her kitchen: DID I SAY THAT OUT LOUD?

Yep, and unfortunately we all get there at times. No matter how much we suppress the things we think about or hide the things we're ashamed of, they somehow slip out of all of us... eventually.

THE TEENAGER SPIRIT

"You know, grandchildren are God's reward for not killing your teenager." That's what an old lady said to me at an event. I laughed so hard when she said this. What a hilarious statement! Now that I have three teenagers, I know what she means.

Teenagers are naturally predisposed to rebel. And they simply can't hide that tendency from anyone. They have what I like to call the teenager spirit. It's adventurous but at times dangerous. They are trying to figure out who they are and to differentiate themselves from their parents. They try to figure out what happens when they cross the lines, and they try to negotiate a new order to live in. I'm looking forward to that day when I get rewarded for these days being a father to teenagers.

However, many of us retain some of that teenager spirit in us, a bit of rebellion against the world around us, and certainly against authority over us, including God. I've seen people who've grown old, but they've never grown up. They may be forty-eight like me, sixty-eight, or even eighty-eight, nearly twice my age. But they still cannot hide that teenager spirit that lurks inside them.

I've been honored to speak all over the world, and almost every time I speak I ask all the men in the audience to raise their hands if they like it when a teenager tells them, "You are the problem in my life, and you need to back off." I ask them to raise a hand and tell me they appreciate the teenager spirit when teens say something like, "Get out of my room, you're ruining my life!" From San Antonio to Singapore, I have never seen one hand raised when I ask this.

I always say this next: "You're like God in that way. You don't like rebellion against you. You don't like the shortsighted, entitled opinion of someone who doesn't know what they're talking about, and is completely disregarding the fact that you have given them everything they have in life. You know it is injustice."

God feels this way about our rebellion, about our entitled opinion that we don't need him, even though he's given us everything and deserves our gratitude. When we don't give God his due, it bothers him just like it bothers us. The teenager spirit irritates us because we are like God; we are made in the image of God. He was like this before we were.

In these settings, I always ask a second question: "Now, if that same teenager, your teenager, were to come back, months or even years after rebelling against you, and say, 'Dad, I'm sorry. I wasn't right to say those things to you. I was ungrateful and I've done things I'm now ashamed of. I don't want to do this anymore. Will you forgive me?'"

I ask these men, "Please raise your hand if you would forgive that teenager, if you would wrap that kid up in your arms and forgive them of everything, because that is the best response you could look for and would mean so much to you?" Each time when I ask this, the hands fly up across the room, whether men are young and without kids or great-great-grandfathers. There are far too many hands to stop and count.

I tell them, "That's because you think like God, too. When your children ask for forgiveness, you want to give grace. It doesn't change what they've said or done; you just want the relationship with them restored. God wants that, too. You're like him; you're made in his image. This is the kind of relationship God wants with you. All he wants is for you to say, 'I'm sorry. I wasn't right to say those things to you. I was ungrateful and I've done things I'm now ashamed of. I don't want to do this anymore. Will you forgive me?'"

Each time, your Father in Heaven wraps you up in his arms and restores that relationship with you. It's how he's wired, just like you.

HIDING

We are tempted to shrug off the things we do that we are ashamed of and say, "I just made a mistake." But you know you've got stuff in your life that amounts to more than simple mistakes. We are talking about intentional actions—things we've all done that we are not proud of. You don't feel that guilty about mistakes, since you didn't do them intentionally.

You might say, "Well, nobody is perfect," and I would say that is a little more on track. These intentional actions, and our tendency to excuse them, are what the Bible calls sin. It's okay to talk about these things. It's not judging you or others. It's just a matter of being honest with God and not hiding the fact that we do these things.

It can offend and hurt you deeply if people commit certain actions against you or someone you love. You also get hurt and feel betrayed when people have let you down and refused to do the loving things you asked them to do. What do you call these offenses that other people commit against you? You would probably call some of them unforgivable. God does hurt, too. And these things that people do or don't do that grieve God's heart are what Scripture calls sin. And fortunately for all of us, God says that our actions against him are forgivable.

The very first people talked about in the Bible sinned. They were provided for by God in every conceivable way, and only one thing was off-limits: eating the fruit of the tree in the center of Eden. Of course, it didn't take long for the first people to be enticed: "the tree was beautiful and its fruit looked delicious."[1] Doing the things we're not supposed to do can seem so *beautiful*, downright *delicious* even. And we believe lies we are told about it, just like the first people who "wanted the wisdom it would give..."

So, they *sinned*. This is just the first in many decisions to do the opposite of what God tells us to do. If I was in that garden instead of Adam and Eve, I would have fallen, too, I'm sure.

But what happened next is what I'm interested in talking to

you about now. After their eyes were opened, they realized they were naked, so they hid from God. After a little hide-and-seek with the Creator of the universe, Adam said, "I was afraid...so I hid."

This is what happens when we sin. It's not just the pattern for Adam and Eve—it's the pattern for all of us. Adam and Eve were simply the first. We do it this way:

First, we *hide*, then we *blame*.

Why did Adam and Eve hide? Because they were experiencing what we all do: *shame*. One Bible translation puts it this way: "...their eyes were opened, and they suddenly felt shame at their nakedness."[2] They realized what they'd done, and so do we at some core level. The only thing we can do is to hide from God, and hide from each other, as Adam and Eve did. It's human nature.

But they still got caught. That's the way it is with God. You can run but you can't hide from someone who is truly omniscient. And no matter how smart we think we are—our "sewn-fig-leaves" level of larceny doesn't provide any God-camouflage.

Now, sometimes our tendency to hide just looks plain silly. Once when my son Colby was being scolded for writing on the walls with crayon, he turned to his mother and asked some pretty serious three-year-old questions. "How do you know I did it? You didn't see me do it. You didn't hear me do it."

It reminds me of several criminals I read about who tried to hide but were eventually found out. In Scotland, a man stole a bottle of vodka, but was caught later. Why? On his way out he asked the clerk for a date and gave her his name and phone number. In North Carolina, several cash registers were stolen from a restaurant. But the cops solved this one easily—since the robber neglected to rip off the white cash register tape, which the police followed some fifty yards next door to the robber's apartment, where he was trying to crack open the registers in his living room. In Minnesota, a man punched a woman in the face after getting into an argument with her. When he was confronted by a bystander, he then attacked that person and ran off, but he dropped a folder he'd had in his hand. The contents of the folder led to the man directly, since the papers had his name on them. What were the papers? His homework from an anger-management class. One presumes he wasn't doing well in that class, either.

We try to hide, but somehow we get caught. If not by the cops, we get caught by God, who knows all.

But here's the amazing thing: God knows everything you've ever done but he still loves you. God knew that Adam and Eve had disobeyed, but he still wanted to be with them. So he confronted them and set the course to make things right. God's love isn't like ours, either, since he's quick to forgive. There were consequences for Adam and Eve, and there are for us as well, but God still wants to cross that barrier and be with us, even as we're attempting to cover ourselves up, fig leaves and all.

We hide even when it's not something we did wrong, but something wrong that's being done to us—when someone else is sinning. That's what the prophet Elijah was facing, in 1 Kings 19. The queen, Jezebel, had threatened to kill him, so he fled in fear and hid in a cave. After providing food and water for him, God asked, "What are you doing here, Elijah?"[3]

Whether you've done something wrong, or something wrong is being done to you, the reaction of us all is to *hide*.

But it doesn't end there. Once we are found, as Adam and Eve were, hiding in the bushes like teenagers, or like Elijah was, hiding in a cave like a criminal on the run, we all tend to do the same thing: blame.

BLAMING

First we hide, then we *blame*.

Adam blamed Eve. Do you see it in that passage? He said, "The woman you put here with me"[4] gave him the fruit, and he just ate it, is all. Then the woman blamed the serpent who tricked her into eating it. Of course, Adam was cryptically blaming God himself, not just Eve, by saying "The woman *you* put here..."

Rather than take responsibility for my actions, it is always tempting to lay the weight of my guilt on somebody else's shoulders. If they had looked at me in a different way, if they had just been nicer or had chosen a different approach, or if they knew I wasn't a morning person, *this* would have never happened! So you see, it's not really my fault.

So, my question for you is twofold: First, how are you *hiding*? Then, who are you *blaming*?

Hiding from God comes in different forms. We keep ourselves busy to hide from God, so stressed we never stop to think and let guilt creep in. We fill our eyes and ears with all kinds of noise and entertainment, so we might not see the hand of God, or hear his voice. We verbalize our justifications to friends for ourselves, and that becomes a story, because in the end we don't just hide from God, or from others: We hide our true selves even from ourselves.

But have you ever felt so tired from the hiding and blaming that you were willing to go a different direction? You just couldn't pass the weight you were carrying off or pretend like it wasn't there anymore.

GOD UNCENSORED

Recently God has worked on me in two big areas. I want to share one of those with you here. On the outside, my life was pretty put together, but no one knew that inside me I carried bitterness about being wronged by someone back in my twenties. The pain from that experience would sporadically resurface in my life. I felt like it was following me around and stalking me like an enemy with a personal vendetta. I remember how it would all too often just get under my skin thinking back to those days of betrayal and hurt. But I was finally tired of fighting.

I couldn't go to the person directly to try to repair things, and I'm not sure if that was the point anyway. I just needed to release the bitterness. The reality is that by this point, I was being held back by inappropriately holding on to things in this way. So, I went back and met with the current pastor of the church where it all went down. I said, "May I come back and ask for your forgiveness?" I told him some of the ugly stuff that had happened and asked for forgiveness and sought freedom.

Now, no lightning flashed across the sky at this. No thunder rolled as a sign of approval from God. It was just done. I moved on. Later that day, my nephew and I went to work out at a fitness center. As I walked in, someone was calling my name, someone who knew me. As I squinted to see who it was, I realized it was the son of the man who had hurt me so badly all those decades ago. We had a great conversation, and I'm sure he has no clue of the history I had with his father—but it was like God was giving me a little gift of letting go and moving on from the bitterness I had carried.

God wasn't done yet, because as I entered the fitness center, one of the men who was involved in the whole situation all those years ago was there, and I got to have a very healthy conversation with him about that era that caused so much bitterness in me for so long. It was as if God were saying to me: "I brought you back here to get closure on this stuff, Todd, so just let it go."

No one knew the bitterness in my heart, but the all-knowing God knew. After this, my relationship with God improved, and my relationship with others did, too. All along, God knew the damage he could heal me from. I finally let him. What a better option than hiding or blaming!

PETER'S DENIAL

We just talked about Peter, but I would like to share some details we missed in the last chapter.

Before Peter ever denied Jesus, Jesus gave Peter the whole scoop. Jesus even put a timer on the "sin" Peter was about to commit. "Before the rooster crows twice, you will deny three times that you even know me."[5]

Of course Peter argued with Jesus: "Even if I have to die, I would never betray you." Peter had that same teenager spirit we find in ourselves. But Peter had nothing he could hide from Jesus. Neither do we.

As the situation with Peter shows us, God knows all the sins we've done, all the sins we're doing now, and even all the sins we're going to do. He knows all this but still chooses to forgive us and keep on restoring us if we just humbly take responsibility for our sins and ask him to help us turn from them.

6

CHURCHIANS

Is it okay that I don't like hypocritical church people?
Is there any defense for how they treat people?

S he was petite, polite, and dressed business casual as she stepped outside the front door of her small but nice starter home to meet my pastor friends.

There from her front porch she could see the big cross standing out in front of the church near where my friends had come from. The cool but clear September evening didn't hinder the chance for conversation, either.

My friends asked her for her permission to help with a brief five-minute survey, as they were gathering information to help them care better for the neighbors living around their church.

After three years of meeting and greeting people at their doorsteps, the pastors had decided on a list of three questions. The first: What's the most important thing a person could know about God? The second: What's been your biggest spiritual experience? And the third: Do you ever think about Heaven and whether you are going there? These days people don't often want to talk to others on their doorsteps, but perhaps this was a different day.

Rather quickly, the young lady agreed and was willing to participate.

Then came the first question. "What's the most important thing a person could know about God?" She froze. Her smile disappeared, and her face hardened. Not loudly but firmly she said, "I'll pass." My friends were not ready for that answer. For out of the possible fifteen hundred doors where they had already asked that question, nobody had ever just "passed."

Not sure what to say next, they asked the second question. "What's been your biggest spiritual experience?"

Trying to hold back tears, the lady began to tremble and then spoke. "Three years ago, my husband died. It was suicide. And my church said, 'Christians don't do that,' and they kicked me out."

My friends were stunned. The third question was never asked. Tears were now rolling down all three faces on that little porch. The pain that came from that God-loved young widow was unbearable for all of them to handle. An atrocity had been committed against both this woman and God.

My friends felt a knot of grief that only God could share with them at that moment. They tried to express how sorry they were for what had happened to this hurting young lady but soon left her doorstep figuratively slapped in the face by what a "church" had done to her. They couldn't even talk to each other as they walked all the way back to their church, unable to visit another front door that night.

To make matters even worse, in the short dialogue that did

occur after the woman's painful but bitterly honest response was the communicated assumption that the church was a congregation her family had grown up in and had attended for years, a church likely including family members.

How could that even happen? Don't Christians know that Jesus didn't do that to people? He didn't kick people who were down and out.

Hidden hurts are often the most difficult to help anyone with. And suicides are most often the worst and most confusing pain a family experiences at the hand of someone they loved. I am sure that this woman probably was the person most surprised and deeply hurt by her young husband's suicide.

Jesus let people with deep hurts touch him and he touched them all the time. Jesus would have supported her, cried with her, and lifted up this broken, twenty-something, grieving widow.

Wouldn't the true church of Jesus do the same?

HYPOCRITES

The messes that churchgoers create are enormous. I find it painful to use the word *Christian* to describe some people's behavior today. Obviously many churches are made up of legitimate followers of Christ. They are honest, caring, and Christ-following, but not perfect. The other group that seems to spend a lot of time in the media these days is nothing like the first one. These people are just pretending to be Christians. They have added a few rules that Jesus never mentioned or they at least have abandoned the grace and compassion that Jesus showed to all people. I like to call this second group what they are, Churchians. I think it's so ironic that Churchians are so afraid of other religions. The real threats to the message of Christ are people who painfully misrepresent Jesus to this hurting and confused world.

Take my grandmother, for example. Years ago, she was working with the youth in a very conservative small church where she lived. She liked being involved with her daughters, and my mother and aunt both have some fond memories of those days.

But then a group of ladies became crosswise with my grandmother because she wore a wedding ring, which, at the time, was a matter of obscure controversy for these conservative people who questioned the wearing of "unnecessary jewelry." They conspired together and forced the pastor to address the issue. He put my grandmother on notice, telling her she would have to either remove her wedding ring or attend church elsewhere.

I see myself as responsible for making right that wrong in my own church. Churchians have no right to dispense such false judgment. It has deep consequences.

What would Jesus have said about my grandmother and the widowed woman my friends talked to? In the book of Matthew, Jesus didn't mince words about this kind of activity among the religious. He used his most dire warning for those who would shut someone out of the Kingdom of Heaven: "What sorrow awaits you teachers of religious law and you Pharisees. Hypocrites! For you shut the door of the Kingdom of Heaven in people's faces. You won't go in yourselves, and you don't let others enter either."[1] If you're fed up with hypocrites among the religious, then you have the same attitude Jesus had. He was fed up with this two thousand years before you were.

Many who are treated badly by a church start to doubt God and their faith. Some even consider switching their religion to another. I would say this to you: Don't switch your faith, just switch your church.

Seriously, I'm not afraid to say that if people are acting like this in your church, then move on. God doesn't call you to stay faithful to a people who are not faithful to him. It's not your job to take others with you or take potshots at them on your way out (then you'd be doing what they do). Instead, just get to a healthy place where people are truly like Christ. Life is too short to spend it all with Churchians.

CHURCH PEOPLE

Because of my work in recent years, I've had the privilege to travel all over the place and talk to all kinds of people—many of whom are not in the church and haven't been for some time. I hear this consistent theme from them: "How can I trust God when I know I can't trust so many church people?"

I want to talk to you about church people and trusting God. If you are bothered by the hypocrisy of the church, or have trouble understanding how Jesus can be all he's cracked up to be when his followers are so messed up sometimes, then we have a lot to talk about.

So, you think *you* have problems with church people. Get this: I'm a pastor, so I'm around these people all the time! I've got *way* more problems with church people than you do. I love working with people who come to church to offer their lives to Christ. They want to learn. They want to serve. They even seem to enjoy God. But Churchians usually like the other people in the church to give their lives to them, especially the pastor.

I'm done defending myself to these kinds of people. You might as well change the word PASTOR on the church office door to OFFICE OF COMPLAINTS because I've received every kind of complaint in the book through the years from church people. They sound like this:

> *Your kids aren't acting like they should.*
> *Your wife isn't wearing what she should wear.*
> *The preaching isn't deep enough for the mature Christians here.*
> *The preaching isn't accessible enough to new people here.*
> *Your house is too nice. Not appropriate for a minister.*
> *Your landscaping needs some help. Makes the church look bad.*
> *A pastor shouldn't drive a super-nice truck like that. Wasteful.*
> *You need to spend more time doing _____ and less doing*
>
> *_____ .*

I've seen those two blanks filled in with everything under the sun. The nice part about pastoring in the same place for two decades is that you start to hear the same stuff over and over and it doesn't shock you like it used to. You just brush it off and move on to the work that matters.

I even get grief about not wearing ties all the time. Here's the thing: I'm short and stocky, a little guy with a thick neck and short arms. Ties choke me because I can't button the top collar of the short shirts I need to wear. I'll wear them for funerals and weddings, but otherwise I'm an open-collar guy. But some people are so obsessed with the little things, they act like I'm disgracing their mother's grave by not wearing a tie when I share a devotional at a prayer meeting.

What really hurts is the fact that I know non-church-people who will rush into a burning building to save someone from a fire. Then I know some church people who, if they saw someone on fire, would only call their pastor to talk about it.

But it's not just me. If you are irritated by these supposedly spiritual types, you're in good company; Jesus was, too.

In chapter 13 of the book of Luke, Jesus healed a woman who had been crippled for eighteen years and couldn't stand up straight. She praised God loudly for this right away. But the religious leader in charge of the place where he was worshipping got angry about the healing because it was done on the holy day. The word used is "indignant" or "very displeased." He nitpicked on this point and said people should come to be healed only on the other six days of the week.

Jesus didn't look the other way. He instead said, "You hypocrites!" and explained that each of them would feed their ox or donkey on that day but then condemn a person who "has been held in bondage by Satan for eighteen years."[2] He was basically saying they were so uptight about their religious rules that they cared more for their donkeys than they did for people God sent them to care for.

Could it be that Jesus would walk up to Churchians today and confront them, accusing them of valuing their own rules and their own pets more than the lives of the people around them? The woman in need in Luke 13 was valued by Jesus. If you or someone you love has ever been minimalized or devalued by someone you suspect to be a Churchian today, Jesus cares much more for you than you might ever know.

TWO SONS

In the book of Matthew, chapter 21, Jesus told the story of a man with two sons. He told the older one to work in the vineyard, and he said he wouldn't, "but later he changed his mind and went anyway."[3] Then he told his younger son to go, too, and—ever respectful—he said, "Yes, sir, I will." But here's the catch—the second son didn't go at all.

So, Jesus asked the "leading priests and elders"[4] who were there to challenge him, "Which of the two obeyed his father?" These priests and elders replied that it was the older brother, the first, who obeyed. Even though he said he wouldn't go, what mattered is that he went.

Jesus didn't hesitate a moment: "I tell you the truth, corrupt tax collectors and prostitutes will get into the Kingdom of God before you do. For John the Baptist came and showed you the right way to live, but you didn't believe him, while tax collectors and prostitutes did. And even when you saw this happening, you refused to believe him and repent of your sins."[5]

This is a big deal. These leading priests and elders were the most spiritually powerful people in all of Jesus' land at the time. They were like the bishops, church denominational presidents, and superintendents of their day. They dictated truth and interpreted Scripture, and they were not used to being challenged on anything, much less being told that they were wrong about obeying God.

What's more, Jesus pointed out that the lowest of the low—the "corrupt tax collectors and prostitutes"—were more obedient than they were, and would enter Heaven ahead of them. This is astonishing! These leading priests and elders couldn't imagine someone more unethical, thieving, and disturbing than a Roman-government-colluding, corrupt tax collector. They couldn't imagine someone more disgusting and vile than the prostitute selling her body in dark alleys.

Jesus, however, saw things differently. He knew that if you put a corrupt businessman on one side, who knew that he was wrong and then changed his ways and started to follow Jesus, and a religious man who harbored secret evil no one knew about on the other side, then the businessman was closer to God. He knows that a twenty-five-year-old stripper strung out on heroin who comes to a point of seeking Jesus and begins to change her ways is closer to God than the religious woman who looks down her nose at every young woman she meets, judging herself to be better than them at every turn.

Jesus makes it clear: Religion is not the point. He's not here to start a new religion, he's here to start a revolution, and he'll begin outside the super-spiritual religious types. Religion is a social reality in every society. He's here to do something entirely different.

It was already predicted in Isaiah 43:19 . . .

"For I am about to do something new. See, I have already begun! Do you not see it? I will make a pathway through the wilderness. I will create rivers in the dry wasteland."[6]

So, here's the surprise for you if you don't trust the religious ones. You're in good company: Jesus didn't trust them, either. What's more, Jesus cares most about your actual obedience—your actions that prove you're following him. He isn't looking for a membership card or a record of showing up and sitting in a room to prove you follow him. He's not looking for people who *say* they are going to work in the vineyard; he's looking for those who *show up*, even if they said they wouldn't before.

If you are sacrificing for other people, doing something for the community, then you are on the right track. You are closer to the kingdom of God than you think.

LIKE US OR LIKE JESUS

The word *Christian* has an interesting origin. In Acts, the account in the Bible of the early church, it talked about Barnabas and Paul, early apostolic leaders. Barnabas went to get Paul, who had converted to Jesus dramatically after hating the church more than anyone alive. He took him to the city of Antioch, and the book said, "Both of them stayed there with the church for a full year, teaching large crowds of people."[7] (It was at Antioch that the believers were first called Christians.)

So, the word *Christian* just means "like Christ." These people were known for their actions, and thus associated with Jesus. It stuck. It makes sense. But understand this: Jesus didn't invent the term *Christian*. Even the church itself didn't have some branding meeting with flip charts and decide this was their new name, unveiling a logo and a website. It was what *the world* called *the church*.

Here's the deal: The term *Christian* is a title you earn, not one you self-proclaim. Don't worry about Churchians who call themselves Christian. That doesn't matter in the least to Jesus. Look for the people who prove themselves to be "like Christ." Those are the real deal; those are the ones who prove God is for real in their lives.

The problem is when people start to flip it around. They don't trust Jesus because they think Jesus is "like us"—meaning, "like the church." That's not how it works. Even a great church that is trying to be more and more like Jesus isn't a true representation of Jesus Christ. They will fail you eventually, too. Jesus isn't like the church, but true Christians are becoming more like Christ.

THE PROMISES OF GOD

So, don't worry about saying yes to the church first. Say yes to Jesus. Become more and more like him. Show up to the vineyard he sends you into, whatever that looks like, by obeying him in your community, making a difference.

You can trust God, even if you don't think you can trust his people yet. You can trust him, the Bible says, "because of his glory and excellence"...because "he has given us great and precious promises. These are the promises that enable you to share his divine nature and escape the world's corruption caused by human desire."[8] His promises are intense and so meaningful for your life. Can I share a few with you?

- **God promises to listen to you.** Do you ever feel like nobody much listens to you? Do have trouble being truly heard? No one listens like God. The Bible says, "'For I know the plans I have for you,' says the Lord. 'They are plans for good and not for disaster, to give you a future and a hope. In those days when you pray, I will listen.'"[9] If you haven't tried praying before, then just start talking to God, even yelling and complaining if that's where you need to start. You may feel a sense of silence at first—but that's good. So much better than all those who don't listen, who talk over your words, who only listen so they can start saying what they want to say. God is a listener.

- **God promises to carry you.** He won't leave you alone if you're falling. He'll be there to the end. The Bible says, "I will be your God throughout your lifetime—until your hair is white with age. I made you, and I will care for you. I will carry you along and save you."[10] Wow . . . this is the kind of support you get from your Creator. Let him carry you when you think you cannot go on. That's someone you can trust!

- **God promises to give you rest.** Do you ever feel like you can't get true rest? You have days off or vacations, but there's some tiredness bone-deep inside you that no one can cure. That's the rest God gives. His Bible says, "Then Jesus said, 'Come to me, all of you who are weary and carry heavy burdens, and I will give you rest.'"[11] You may have some seriously heavy burdens, but he is ready to cure that weariness and finally give you the spiritual rest you need.

STARTING NARRATIVE

You hear a lot these days about narrative—the narrative of a political party, the media narrative, the Hollywood narrative. It seems like two different leaders can look at the same facts and have a different narrative, a different story line.

I must admit that the church sometimes drifts into this habit as well. A friend in my church, John, told it to me this way: "Before I knew God, I would look at all the churches in town, and the way I figured it, everyone that went to those churches saw that each church had their own rules and they just ended up choosing a church that matched their lifestyle and then they teach what you like." Yikes—this is not the way church life is supposed to be! Denominations and different churches shouldn't just be a place to line up your predetermined choices in life, so you're perpetually surrounding yourself with others who already agree with everything you say! People need to be looking for and finding churches that will teach them to follow Christ in all things—both the easy and the hard to deal with. This is why I find some small satisfaction when someone disagrees with what I'm preaching in my church. The reality is, I actually don't want them to agree with me all the time; I want to stretch them, not coddle them.

In the end, media, political, or Hollywood narratives do not drive truth. Neither do the Baptist or Lutheran or Catholic or even my own Wesleyan narratives. We need a source for truth that is outside these human-made institutions, whether they are secular or we consider them sacred.

Scripture is where we find that nonsubjective source. You'll notice in this book that I don't merely rely on my opinion; I rely on Scripture. This may be hard for you, as you may not treat the Bible with the reverence I do. But don't give up on it yet. By starting with Scripture, we start with a narrative that is not easy to dismiss as "just another person's opinion." In this day of social media time lines, fake news, and talking heads, we need a place to find unchanging truth.

If you are new to the Bible, please listen carefully to what I have to say next. Don't start with Genesis, please. If you want to stay on the right spiritual track, you need to first learn everything you can about the true Jesus. Start reading with Matthew, Mark, Luke, or John. And do plan to stay awhile; maybe the next-best advice is to read these books several times before you start reading elsewhere.

I want to encourage you to take your focus off the narratives of our society and the hypocrites and Churchians. They are just a distraction to take your attention off the Christ they are supposed to be like but aren't. He comes and asks you to follow him with all your heart. Become what those hypocrites are not. If the corrupt tax collectors and prostitutes are closer to the Kingdom of Heaven than them, then how close are you right now?

THINKING OF ME

I don't think much about God;
does he think much about me?

Ａfter the September 11, 2001, attacks, critical incident stress management training began to spread across our country. I was trained for this work, especially for times when the fire department has a fatality. Fire personnel and policemen everywhere need a place to unload the weight of the tragedies they encounter before their marriages or their very lives implode.

When you see volunteer firefighters, however, you might be tempted to not see them in the same light as the pros. But there is a hard reality to what we do. It is true that we don't respond to the same volume of calls that the pros do, but we do respond to the same *type* of calls. We have to meet the same requirements of training and preparation as any paid department. So our true handle should be "unpaid professionals."

But the hardest thing that sets us apart from the big departments in the big cities is our network. We come from a small town so we often know the people involved in what we are responding to. When we show up on the scene, we often know the victim. Just last night someone I knew flipped her car and died. One of the men in my church worked with her every day and was devastated by her death. All emergency personnel are shaken up by what they see, even when it's a stranger. But when we small-town volunteers show up, the person behind the wheel usually isn't a stranger.

Imagine this situation from our fire department in years past: A group of firefighters are in the first fire truck onto the scene of a rollover, and when they find the car wreck they know right away who the fatality is. It's their buddy's kid, and he's a fireman, too, responding a truck or two behind them. So, they're calling back to the command vehicle on their cell phone to discreetly try to call the other fire truck off—because he just can't see this yet. His six-year-old is lying lifeless among the wreckage. I'm crying right now thinking of that situation; there are no words for it.

That's the kind of thing a small-town fireman must deal with.

GOD EVERYWHERE

One of the greatest honors I have in life is also one of the hardest duties of my life. I serve as the state fire chaplain. This means that when there is an in-the-line-of-duty death of one of our emergency fire response personnel, I often go to the funeral and represent all firemen in the state of Nebraska. I do funerals as a pastor all the time, but line-of-duty funerals are a complete contrast with the average funeral service. Even as I was working on this chapter, I had just been to one of those funerals. A man had died in the line of duty, serving his community. Nothing out of the ordinary; the pager indicated that an ambulance needed to respond to a local residence. No flames. No smoke. No broken glass or wreckage. But still enough stress to trigger an abnormality in a young thirty-something man's heart. His family didn't even get to say good-bye.

After the packed funeral at the fire station, I spoke at the committal, which is when we take the body to the grave. There, the family must say their final good-byes over the casket. All deaths are hard, but these are always tragic, honoring someone who was heroic but now is gone.

For a line-of-duty death, the committal is a bigger deal than other funerals. There are fire trucks and a lineup of firefighters in dress uniform. Often two fire trucks will blast their water cannons into the air, crossing them for visual effect while bagpipes simultaneously play "Amazing Grace."

When I see all this, I'm reminded that while you might not see this kind of public support and affirmation at your loved one's funeral, God does give you the same amount of attention as any individual hero some other family buries. God pays just as much attention to the ones our public overlooks as to the ones they honor. God thinks of you, or your grandma and grandpa, more than you are thinking of him.

You know, many firemen I've talked with through the years don't go to church, but I think I'd rather talk to firefighters than many of the people who do go to church week after week and don't listen. Much like a husband might be accused of tuning out his wife, I know many who have tuned out their pastor. I've had unchurched firemen come up and repeat to me exactly what I told them from the Bible three months before, verbatim. God is at work.

I often read from Psalm 139[1] at these kinds of committal services, which is one of the most beautiful passages in the Bible. I think this passage speaks to the main point I want to make in this chapter, so take some time to read those verses with me, thinking about how God knows each of us.

When we think of God, we often think of his qualities of bigness in terms of the universe, in terms of planets and solar systems and creation. But what makes God most powerful, what makes God most real, is the fact that the Creator of all things takes the time to notice you and me. The Psalmist who wrote Psalm 139, most likely King David, put it this way: "You have searched me, Lord, and you know me." God's knowledge is not just of the things that are eternal; it is of the things inside you and me.

This includes my very thoughts: "You perceive my thoughts from afar. You discern my going out and my lying down; you are familiar with all my ways." In fact, before I say something, before "a word is on my tongue," Psalm 139 says God knows it "completely."

This is hard to understand. Honestly, it makes my brain hurt to think of all that is in God's brain. Psalm 139 says it this way: "Such knowledge is too wonderful for me, too lofty for me to attain."

King David began to wonder about how he could even escape

the careful protective attention of God. Could he run from God? No, he could never escape that presence. "If I go up to the heavens, you are there; if I make my bed in the depths, you are there. If I rise on the wings of the dawn, if I settle on the far side of the sea, even there your hand will guide me, your right hand will hold me fast." God is not only present in all these places but there to guide you, to hold you fast and protect you.

This is a big deal. God's there with you on an airplane or in a submarine, he's there if you stand on a mountain in Japan, looking to the bright sunrise, and he's there with you if you travel to Alaska to watch the last sunset that starts a long hard winter.

These days I'm noticing a lot of talk about a staffed mission to Mars. It seems that human beings want to become, as they are saying, an "interplanetary species." Well, guess what: If my great-grandkids someday are so advanced that they are colonizing Mars, if they stand on a mountain on Mars and look for the sunrise on that great red ball—God is there, too. We can never, and will never, flee from God.

GOD'S ATTENTION TO THE LITTLE THINGS

This is a quality about God that I love: God's bigness doesn't affect his attention to detail, to the little things in your life. Big things start to become so large you almost can't comprehend them. If you stand looking at the Grand Canyon, it is so big that the distances don't even make sense. If you blocked both ends of the canyon, it would take 1.1 quadrillion gallons of water to fill it. If you didn't block it, you would have to flood much of the entire earth to overtop the edges of that canyon. That scale is hard to comprehend.

In February 2016, Riccardo Sabatini gave a TED Talk about the human genome, the entire genetic code of a single human being. At one point, he pulled quite a stunt: He invited Craig Venter, the first man to sequence human DNA, to join him on stage. But instead of the man in the flesh, five assistants pushed out library carts stacked with huge books.

Sabatini explained that it wasn't Venter in the flesh, but "for the first time in history, this is the genome of a specific human, printed page by page, letter by letter—262,000 pages of information." In 175 books, they had printed a human, or at least the data that makes up a human. On stage, Sabatini read eight letters, the eye color of the scientist, and then another set of letters that—if they were in a different order—would mean Venter had cystic fibrosis.

This is how complex I am, and how complex you are. But God understands it all. He is big enough to fill the Grand Canyon, and personal enough to know every single letter and its order in your genetic code, weaving it together as David said in Psalm 139: "For you created my inmost being; you knit me together in my mother's womb. I praise you because I am fearfully and wonderfully made; your works are wonderful, I know that full well. My frame was not hidden from you when I was made in the secret place, when I was woven together in the depths of the earth. Your eyes saw my unformed body; all the days ordained for me were written in your book before one of them came to be."

Further proof of how big and real God is can be found in

the fact that the intimate knowledge and love he has for us is not focused on just one of us. He loves you with the exact same force and energy that he loves me. Many have said, "God loves each of us as if there is only one of us."

As a father, I noticed that for my kids, I was always the measuring stick to compare things with. Even when my son had his experience in Heaven that we recounted in the prior book, he would compare everything with me. He would say that a sword was as tall as I was, or that a certain angel was twice as tall as me.

Now, of course, my kids know that I am not that big—that their dad is actually short. They've seen my short height, my short temper, my short vision, and my short wisdom at times. But they also have the real Heavenly Father to compare things with now. They have God. He's truly big in every way that I fall short.

I think it's an act of worship to say that God is big and real. If we can just back away from our selfishness, we will discover that God has put in us the potential to do amazing things. Most of God's love, values, and righteousness are similar to what we want to see in the world when we are on the right track.

CANADIAN NEWS SHOW AGNOSTIC

I was on a news show in Canada one time and the producer warned me, "In Canada, we can't just put you on the show; we have to have both sides so there is some debate." I didn't know what he was talking about, but I just played along. So, they put an agnostic person on the show with me, and after I shared some of my story, he started to "debate" me.

Here's the thing about a debate—you must have two people engaging for it to really be a debate. I'm not much for debates. And I was sure that debating this guy wasn't going to change his mind or the minds of any viewers. Instead, all those already inclined to think like him would just agree with him and think I was an idiot, and vice versa for folks already inclined to think like me. Therefore, much of debate-style television doesn't make a difference in the world today.

So, I just asked one question of the guy: "Are you honest?"

He hesitated, clearly caught off-guard, and carefully but not boldly said, "Of course."

I told him, "Well, if you're honest, go home today and pray an honest prayer like this: 'God, if you're real, I know you know I'm being honest with you right now. I am asking you if you are for real, and if Jesus is your son. I'm asking you to show that to me if it's true.'"

God answers this prayer. That's why Scripture repeats again and again, "You will seek me and find me when you seek me with all your heart."[2] We don't need to have all the answers; we just need to ask people to ask God for the answers, and he'll provide them. Time after time I have seen God deliver on this prayer, if you pray it honestly.

REAL ANSWERS TO PRAYER

I became a Christian at just nine years of age. Why? I started asking God things and he started responding to my prayers. This "inner" voice began to connect to my soul and started to challenge me. In the most undeniable but personal way that

God could have spoken to me, he proved he was there. He proved he was real. And he wanted me to respond to him. This skinny, towheaded, bucktoothed, bowlegged nine-year-old mattered to God.

There is one very powerful prayer we can all pray for other people, but we don't often do so. We pray for a sick friend, we pray someone we know will get a job, and we pray they will make it through the loss of a loved one. We pray a list of requests, but this is not often something someone requests of you. But you should still pray it.

Pray this: "God, show yourself as real to them."

That simple prayer is so powerful. It's the best thing to pray for our children, for instance. I would rather my kids see God in their circumstances than have no problematic circumstances in their lives. How much better to have a hard experience but see God, rather than to go through nothing and never see God? I don't pray that all people's experience would be perfect, I pray that they would experience God in their circumstances. Pray that God will show himself as real to those you love. He answers this prayer over and over.

God recently answered this prayer again for my younger son, Colby. When he came back from a youth camp, he approached the kitchen table and asked me a question. "Dad, was your dad ever a pastor?" Surprised, I assured him that he wasn't. He continued, "Well, God told me to tell you something."

"Really?" I asked.

"He told me to tell you that he wants me to be a pastor like you."

I remembered that moment in my own younger years.

When God told me to be a pastor, he told me to tell my mother. From one kitchen to another, I was now having the exact same conversation thirty-five years later. I had just switched roles.

Holding back tears, I assured Colby that he would become a much better pastor than I've ever been able to be. Later, I asked him if God had told him anything else. "Yeah," he responded. "God told me to listen to you. You would teach me." I didn't make it this time; I cried.

FIXING PRINCESS

There's nothing quite like the added chaos and love a dog brings to a home. Princess was our thirteen-year-old black Labrador retriever, and she was a source of great joy and love for us all.

It was Thanksgiving time, and part of her jaw was swollen. I thought it was just an abscessed tooth—the veterinarian agreed. My plan was that over the holiday when we were supposed to be out of town, they could drain it and board her a few days; we'd come back after Thanksgiving with Princess all healed up and back to normal.

While I was driving off to see our family, I got a call from Darcie, our vet. Right away she told me she had bad news about Princess. It wasn't an infected tooth. It was a tumor. It was in her jaw, and behind her eye. It had also attached itself to her brain.

She asked me right then—while I was driving—"Do you want me to let her wake up? I can't do much for her. There's no way to get her back to normal. I can only cut part of it away. What's your decision?"

In that moment, I was feeling the weight of deciding this dog's life. Driving to enjoy Thanksgiving, I knew I had a decision to make that would sour the holiday. Immediately, I remembered Princess's eyes. I don't know what it was about that dog's eyes, but I could read all kinds of emotions in them—perhaps those emotions weren't there and the eyes were just a mirror of my own feelings, but I saw them.

The second set of eyes I saw were my daughter's. She was away at college, and if we put her dog down, she wouldn't ever get to say good-bye. She was coming home in just two short weeks. So, I did what any other dad scared to become the bad guy would do. I paused with a quick prayer in my heart, and said to Darcie, "Cut away what you can, and put her on antibiotics. My daughter is coming home from college in a few weeks, and then she can say good-bye before we put her down when we have to."

I needed the vet to try, but I also needed God to grant my prayer. Just giving the dog some pills or brushing off the problem as if it would go away wouldn't be enough. I needed someone who could send the tumor into reverse. So, the vet got to work, and I prayed the entire Thanksgiving weekend.

We need a big God for the same reason. We have emotional and spiritual toothaches at first, but upon examination they are much deeper, and we find tumors that someone bigger and better than us must tackle. We need God because he can fix what we can't.

Princess recovered from surgery and was a lot better for a while afterward. At this point, Darcie revealed, "I guess I called that one wrong." Seeing Cassie come home and say her good-byes to that dog made it all worthwhile for me.

FAMILY PRAYER

One of the things I've felt led to do is have our family pray together several times a week in the evening. We will do it even if the kids are off somewhere else with friends. That might seem like a waste of time to you, but remember we are in a super-small town, so coming by the house for a few minutes isn't that big a deal for the kids. We just pause for a bit and pray, each of us, out loud. The prayers aren't all that special or planned; we just say what is on our hearts.

Since our kids would have to excuse themselves from other things to come to pray, others would hear about the prayer time, and now and then a friend would ask if they could come, too. So, we've had visitors at our family prayer time. Eventually we came to expect a few "extras" to join us from time to time. Sometimes they would stay quiet and watch; other times they would ask us to pray for them, or even join in praying themselves. I think we often write off younger people as being shallow, but teens are clearly hungry for spiritual things!

One of my daughter's friends—I'll call her Emily—came to one of these prayer times. That first time she told us that she wanted us to pray for her. She was having a horrible time sleeping. I could see that in her bloodshot eyes. She was a nice sweet girl, but clearly exhausted. She had gone to doctors and counselors who had tried to help her. Nothing seemed to work, and she would go days at a time without sleep.

I prayed for her, saying, "God, you know the problem here. The doctors haven't been able to help Emily, and we care about her, and want the best for her. She needs you."

I called her the next day and she still hadn't slept. So, I committed to keep praying. The day after that I checked in again, and she was so happy to report that she had finally slept peacefully the night before. A breakthrough had begun in her sleep patterns.

She came to the same family prayer time a week later. "I've got something else to ask you all to pray for, is that okay?"

Emily listened to God and made a commitment to Christ not long after that, and began participating in our youth group. I'm convinced that those simple but desperate prayers turned her life toward Christ.

HEAVEN BY FAVOR

I don't pray for animals much ever, but I sure prayed for Princess that Thanksgiving, that she would make it to my daughter's return at Christmas break. God answered that prayer. Her quality of life improved for a while. The kids spent time with her, saying good-byes and getting closure.

Two months later, Princess stopped swallowing her medicine, and stopped eating and drinking. Her eyes were sunk way back in her head. When I looked into her sad eyes I could tell, and if you've ever been in this situation with a pet, you know that look. She and I both knew it was time.

"Who wants to go with me to the vet?" I had no takers. Sonja refused. Colton declared he was busy. Colby just said, "No way!" They all looked at me as if they were saying, *Nope, Dad, this is your job*. I had to go alone, but I sure didn't want to.

My youngest son lowered the tailgate as I picked up Princess. She was so much lighter now than when I had lifted her up just two months before. What could I say? He was just twelve years old, a full year younger than the dog. She was the only dog he'd known in our home in his entire life. I just prayed these words through tears with my son: "God, thank you for the time we've had with Princess. I know you talk about animals in Heaven, so that gives us faith. I don't know how dogs get to Heaven, but this one, Lord, we'd really like to see again."

God cares about the smallest details in our lives. He listens to what might seem to be the smallest of prayers. What breaks the hearts of our children breaks our hearts—and the same is true for God. Our pain is painful for him to watch. You don't have to be a hero or a pastor or a teenager for God to think about you. He made you. You were his thought to begin with, and you're still in his thoughts even now. But I also know that God has had his hand directing and creating all life—dogs, too!

Mark Twain is noted as saying, "Heaven goes by favor. If it went by merit, you would stay out and your dog would go in."[3] I was so grateful for favor in that moment, so thankful I'll make it to Heaven. But that dog was more faithful, more loving, and more positive than I've ever been. She believed that people, especially kids, were made to pet her. More people in my town like my dog than like me, I'm afraid.

But perhaps God is paying attention to this little detail in my life, and he will give me another thing I don't deserve, and that's to see Princess again in Heaven someday, playing with my kids again.

8

THE SNAKE STILL STRIKES

I get it that people do bad things, but isn't that just the way it always is?

Few things are more enjoyable for me than heading off with a group of guys on a hunting trip. It may seem odd to you, but in recent years we've had fun with wild-pig hunting. We have all hunted other animals, large and small, but wild pigs are fun for us to hunt because they are not restricted like other game—they have been labeled both destructive and dangerous. Their rate of reproduction is also rabbitlike. A feral sow can deliver two litters of out-of-control piglets each year. Today there are a million and a half of these hogs living in the wild in Texas alone.

Even if you're not a hunter, you can imagine it's fun to get away and just be a guy and hang out in the wild. As an added plus, cell reception is pretty poor out there, so we can truly disconnect. Most of the guys on these trips are personal friends, like-minded, and ready for a getaway.

One new friend I met on a hog hunt recently was an active

Navy SEAL. He was tight-lipped and never talked about his duties in the military. He never bragged, or needed to for that matter. His muscles had muscles, and none of us could shoot a rifle at the distances that he could reach. But like us, he needed the break. His friendliness made me once again appreciate all of our military personnel and the sacrifices they make that they can't talk about. Many are just regular guys and gals doing very hard things.

On that trip, I was out by myself at one point trying to find one of those wild hogs when I had a unique experience. It was early in the morning, shortly after sunrise. I wasn't having any luck so, bored, I wandered off the road into the brush littered with cacti and mesquite. Needles are everywhere in that Texas terrain. You have to step very carefully if you don't want to get poked by a vast array of nature's barbed wires. And fortunately for me, stepping very carefully also meant stepping very quietly.

I don't know if you believe in guardian angels or not, but something or someone got my attention. Almost as if someone hit me on the back of the head, I was suddenly compelled to look down at the bottom of the mesquite tree I had just approached. And there coiled under the mesquite was a perfectly camouflaged rattler. Given its diameter I knew it was much bigger than the rattlers I see back home in Nebraska. I had seen snakes this large sleeping in zoos, but I had never before been this close to a sleeping rattlesnake without a wall of glass between us.

I froze. I could feel my heart beating so violently, I was sure I was about to wake this poisonous reptile. A rattlesnake can typically strike about two-thirds of its length, so I knew I needed several feet of separation to escape its strike zone. I could feel the blood draining from my face as I slowly reversed my steps. The rifle in my hand would be useless, as the scope mounted on it was zeroed for two hundred yards, not this two-foot distance. As quietly as possible, I switched the rifle to my left hand while I used my right hand to reach for the revolver on my right hip.

Now, I love shooting rocks off the top of fence posts with my favorite revolver back home. Accuracy takes practice. But when I'm aiming at rocks, I am calm, breathing, and confident. I also get to enjoy a steady two-handed stance. None of those benefits accompanied me as I aimed my sights at the sleeping head of that snake while I slowly stepped backward.

And then…the snake's eyes opened. I was probably far enough back to be safe, but watching those eyes open caused me to react before the snake could. I squeezed the .357 mag's trigger, firing right at the snake's head. The snake slowly slithered a few inches and then stopped moving. I got out of there as fast as I could. Later, I found out that the bullet had nearly separated the snake's head from the rest of its body.

How do I know? Well, back to that Navy SEAL.

BACK TO PROVE IT

When he heard about my snake encounter, he wanted to go retrieve the snake and take a look at it. Um, gross. Snakes and I just don't mix. I wanted no part of going back, but then there was that "prove it" moment. We have all been there, second-guessing the story from the fisherman about the size of the fish he just caught. As I looked at my new friend, I knew I was stuck. I had to prove both myself and my story. So, I agreed to take him back to the snake, but only under two conditions: I wouldn't have to touch it or eat it.

He looked for several minutes under the mesquite before he saw the snake, blending in with the needles and various other forms of Texas debris, lifeless. He grabbed the snake with the snake grappler from the hunting truck. It looked massive to me as he lifted it out from under the bush. I know I'm only five foot six, but once the rattler was laid out on the ground, this snake was definitely beyond my height.

Cutting off what was still attached of the snake's head was job number one. Then we examined my bullet's impact point. Without a shovel to bury the head, my friend kicked it safely back under the bush where the snake came from. But the worst thing ever happened next.

As my friend used the grappler in his hand to count the rattles in the snake's tail, the headless snake that had been dead for close to an hour suddenly moved with lightning speed as it struck at the shaft of the grappler touching its tail. At that point, I about puked. I always thought there were just two types of snakes: live and dead. At that moment, I realized I was wrong. Evidently there are three types of snakes: live, dead, and long dead.

After this encounter and a little snake research on my part, I discovered that some species of venomous snakes might be able to strike for up to nine hours after they are either killed or die naturally. Much like a fish that flops out of water, the nervous system in a snake causes its muscles to still slither and strike. Some sources estimate that about 50 percent of all snakebites happen because people are unaware that dead snakes can still strike.

Later, as I thought back on this experience, I could see how sin works just like a rattlesnake. The thing that once tempted you and even seems dead in you still strikes. Like the snake I shot in Texas, sin's muscle fibers still twitch toward the wrong. Have you ever had that experience? I sure have. I've thought that I had taken something out—been totally victorious over it—but then gone back and done it again, as if it was still alive in the grave.

Sin is like all addictions—alcohol, hoarding, smoking, lust—and as so often happens, people who get clean end up going back to the thing they knew was destroying their life.

The Bible talks about this old dead self in Romans 6, saying, "We know that our old sinful selves were crucified with Christ so that sin might lose its power in our lives. We are no longer slaves to sin."[1] When that old dead head of sin strikes back, the Scripture encourages us, "Do not let sin control the way you live; do not give in to sinful desires."[2]

THE CLEVELAND AIRPORT

I was driving with a friend to a museum in Ohio and we were talking about some heavy stuff. I confessed to him what I'll confess to you now: I've had a huge struggle with lust starting in high school. My big sin snake, the one I just can't seem to kill, is lust. I've seen all kinds of things I wish I had never seen, both when I was younger and as an adult. But even after I wised up, I found that it is hard to escape how pornographic our culture has become.

When Colton was just three years old, that same weekend we talked about in *Heaven Is for Real* when he became sick and went into the hospital, we were in the Greeley Mall in Colorado. He was skipping through the mall, some fifteen or twenty feet ahead of us. We walked past a lingerie store. He walked by a huge poster of a woman wearing mostly nothing. Then he stopped and turned around, pointing at the poster, and said, "Mom, she needs to get some clothes on." Yep, the three-year-old was right. You can't walk through the mall or visit a news website without images being thrown in your face that wouldn't have been deemed acceptable even fifteen years ago. We say things are "not appropriate for under eighteen" when in reality they aren't appropriate for us at any age.

My lust went beyond just the bad stuff I saw, however. I found that thoughts would plague my mind at the most random times, even when I was trying to pray or was in a worship service. I started to feel like I was targeted with them—like I couldn't escape; it was uncontrollable. You can protect yourself from seeing some things, like avoiding that poster my son was bothered by in the Greeley Mall, but you can't protect yourself from your own brain! Like a cold virus that might cause you to cough sporadically, I had a brain virus that would flash distracting images onto the screen of my mind. I had to constantly hit the erase button and refocus.

I confessed all of this to a close friend, telling him that I was just plain sick of it. I had heard many explain that what was happening in my head was normal. "Just the way it is." It was somehow every man's battle till he died; perhaps then he'd experience freedom from it. Well, that didn't give me much hope. I wanted freedom from it in this life.

My friend listened well, and the very first thing he asked me was if I had seen pornography. I said, "Yes, of course. Who hasn't seen pornography is this world?" Then he asked me how old I was when I had first been exposed to it. I had no idea, and just told him it must have been when I was young. He told me he would start praying right then that God would reveal to me the first time I'd seen such a thing. So, he did.

As we continued to drive, his prayer was answered. God popped a memory right into my head, just out of the blue. Apparently, my friend's prayer for me opened me up for God to move. I remembered a time when I was just eight years old. This was a memory I hadn't thought about for decades, a sudden unexpected jolt. After my grandfather died, my grandma started working cleaning hotel rooms. I would help her out when I was visiting her. I'd go into the room ahead of her while she was doing the final deep clean on the last room, and I would take out the trash, strip off the dirty linens, and things like that. Then she would join me and we'd finish the room together.

One time I went into one of these rooms and it had been pretty much trashed—which was a sight I was used to. But on the television stand was a sight that was new to me. It was a glossy magazine with a woman on the cover. I picked it up and started looking through it. I didn't know what I was looking at, other than that it was strange and wrong, but somehow I kept looking. And that was the first time I remember seeing pornography. I told my friend this, and he immediately prayed for me. Then we entered some heavier traffic and our conversation stopped. I didn't feel any change, but was glad he was praying.

We visited the museum, then continued on to our next appointment. Two days later, my friend and two others met up again in the Cleveland airport. We gathered up before the security line, formed a circle, and prayed before our trip home.

During this time, holding hands with the people next to me, I started to hear the friend whom I'd confessed to start praying just for me. I felt a surge of energy come over me as he prayed that God would deliver me from my constant battle with lust. He prayed that from all the way back when I was young till now, God would remove things from my mind, and not let me be distracted by them in my work.

It wasn't some magical prayer, but it was an effective and special one. If I hadn't been holding the hands of those next to me I would have fallen over right there, but holding on kept me up. It was as if Jesus was giving me special power in that moment. I felt like something new had covered me right then and there.

The strangest thing happened. It stuck. I am a changed man now. I don't get interrupted by those images in my mind. Those random temptations don't play over in my mind again and again. Instead, I have the freedom I was always looking for.

The best part is how powerful my times of prayer now feel. I'm not clouded by random temptations, and I'm not constantly having to do battle within myself to keep my attention on the good instead of the bad. God had to be the one to do this, as it was impossible on my own: to truly kill the sin snake in my heart.

Am I impervious to looking at pornography? No. I still have all the same safeguards and more in my life, because I do wonder if it would all come flooding back if I opened that door again. But I do have the freedom now in this life that for decades I longed for!

CONSEQUENCES

What comes to mind when you think of a volunteer firefighter on a Saturday afternoon? Is it a big and burly man with a bit of a stubble beard? Is he sitting on his back porch, maybe sipping a beer while he gets the grill going for the family? Yep, that pretty much describes a lot of the firefighters I know.

Then again, our volunteer fire department has a no-alcohol policy, meaning the guy who decides to have a beer with his hot dog knows that when there is a crisis in our town involving a fire, he can't hop in his truck, put a light on it, and race to the scene. Why?

Imagine how bad it would be if a firefighter crashed a fire truck on the way to an accident—or worse yet, struck a child chasing a ball into the street in the path of our truck. That could cause more damage than the fire itself, and then the truck also wouldn't be there to help with the fire. The public backlash would also be huge, almost impossible to recover from. So we have our policy. Because sometimes the consequences of an action are much greater than we can imagine at the time.

We have policies about driving to a crisis in general, too. We firefighters know that at sixty miles an hour, you cannot hear sirens coming until we are too close to you to make any difference. Our lights and sirens ask for *permission* to get the right-of-way, but it's not a *license* to. Did you know that if someone hits an ambulance in an intersection, usually the law considers it to be the ambulance driver's fault? Driving too fast is one of the biggest temptations along the way to the scene—the adrenaline is pumping and you feel like you gotta get there to respond, so you cut corners, sometimes literally.

A structure fire involves other policies. Each year we get tested for mask fit—if your mask doesn't fit perfectly, in a fire you are going to be exposed to the dangerous toxins in burning carpets or other chemicals. Did you know if a couch in your living room catches fire, you must be out of the house in five minutes to survive? The plates that hold your structure together are going to make that roof crash ten minutes later. We have policies to make sure these scenarios don't occur.

Some sin has dire consequences like these. The greatest agony that churns my stomach is when a pastor is defrocked because of inappropriate behavior, or in some cases arrested. I know we have already talked about Churchians. But when a pastor lets down his guard, commits sinful and unlawful actions against another person or child that God loves, I can almost feel God's pain and hurt.

When children ask me to pray for their parents to get back together and stop fighting, they are often unaware of the infidelity behind the fighting. All I can do is cry with them.

I know many in entertainment and media promote promiscuous lifestyles and open marriages, but please protect yourself and your loved ones. The bite from this snake is venomous. Don't play around with it.

I heard an entertainment industry husband give a pithy statement about the pain he endured separating from his very popular wife and children. He said, "This is so *not* what I wanted!" He was living the life he was encouraged to live, but he didn't like the bite at the end of his decisions.

Whether or not your divorce and hurt are as publicized as this man's pain, let me assure you, I have heard the same statement from hundreds of couples wishing they had protected themselves from marital unfaithfulness and tragedy.

9

THE UNPOPULAR GOD

I get the idea of Heaven, but why talk about Jesus so much?

A news reporter from a Jerusalem newspaper called me one day for a scheduled interview for her paper. She was a nice Jewish woman who spoke English fluently. She had prepared well for our interview, reading my whole book recounting Colton's visit to Heaven. She said she liked it and was looking forward to the movie that was coming. And she had many good questions to ask. It's refreshing to do interviews with people who take the time to do their research. I've been in many conversations where it was obvious that the other person on the end of the phone or the microphone didn't have a clue. The questions that they were asking were just coming from a teleprompter.

Eventually we got to the subject of Jesus, because Colton's experience was centered on Jesus in Heaven. Innocently and plainly, Colton talked in a way that any four-year-old might. But the God he saw was God the Father, God the Son, and

God the Holy Spirit. It can be confusing to us, but it was plain to him. And Jesus was the one he had spent most of his time with.

"You know, Jesus is not the most popular person around here. What should I say to those people here in Jerusalem, so they'll listen to your story?" the reporter asked.

FULFILLED

This was the start of a deeper conversation, because she was so spiritually open. There are many places to start when asked this question, so I started in the beginning. Literally, *the beginning* of the Bible, which opens, "In the beginning God created the heavens and the earth."[1]

I pointed out to her that the focus is not Heaven in the end; it is the God of Heaven. People want to go to Heaven, but my son's experience confirmed which god is the God of Heaven.

I walked through Scripture in the Hebrew Bible, or what most of us call the Old Testament, in contrast with the New Testament in the Christian Bible. The beautiful thing is, Jesus doesn't show up out of the blue. The story stretches for thousands of years before him, and Jews know this. It is *their* story, of course. But it is my story, too—because of Jesus, the Jewish story can become *everyone's* story. This was the plan from the beginning, where Genesis says, "... all peoples on earth will be blessed through you."[2] A few chapters later, God repeats this, saying, "and through your offspring all nations on earth will be blessed, because you have obeyed me."[3] The Hebrew Bible says something similar elsewhere many times, where God promises to the Jews that he "will save you, and you will be a blessing."[4]

It's not hard to walk through how the prophets of the Jews laid things out for Jesus to clearly be the Christ (the Messiah). I've even had conversations with another Jewish friend who was willing to talk about whether Jesus was the Messiah and honestly seek his Scriptures about the subject despite the major challenge it was to his faith. In this case, I don't ask people to keep talking to me or to a rabbi. Instead, I ask them to read the Scriptures and talk to God about it.

"That sounds fair," he responded. He's praying to the right God; he just needs to ask the right God the right questions.

This is true whether you're a Jew or not. It's not about asking advice from a so-called holy man. Instead, as we emphasized in the last chapter, it's important for each of us to pray to God and ask him to show himself to be real. Whether you're an atheist, a Jew, a doubter, a scientist, a Muslim, a Buddhist, or someone who has a mixed-nuts view of faith, it's about you personally approaching God and asking him to make himself real to you.

Isaiah talked of this Messiah being born of a virgin, and the prophet Micah said the birth would take place in Bethlehem. Hosea said the Messiah would come out of Egypt.[5] A massacre was to take place at the birth city of the Messiah, and he would be called a Nazarene and would minister in Galilee.[6] He would be betrayed and mocked.[7] His hands and feet would be pierced.[8] And then people would gamble for his clothes.[9] This is just a sampling of the dozens and dozens of ways that the Hebrew Bible chronicles their prophets talking about Jesus. They prophesied who the Messiah would be—and it was hard to understand, and didn't fit anyone until Jesus came.

I walked through some of these same Scriptures in the Hebrew Bible with this Israeli news reporter who was calling me from just a few miles away from the very places Jesus walked. Now, I am a plainspoken guy and didn't use any special words really, I just told her how her Hebrew Bible pointed to Jesus in all these ways. The Christmas and Crucifixion stories show how the Messiah is certainly Jesus. She was taken aback by all this and said, "I've never seen anything like what you're showing me before."

"Well, the next time you read your Scriptures, could you not just ask yourself if they sound like they are talking about Jesus?" I replied.

I also asked her, "Do you believe God would bless a story like this if I had made it up?" Whatever beliefs she held about God, one was of awareness. She knew that God knew if Colton was representing the truth or not. She said, "No, I don't think so."

I said, "So, you're calling me in Imperial, Nebraska, from Jerusalem, Israel. How does something like this get to you without God propelling it?"

"It doesn't," she said.

If God wanted to, he could have stopped Colton's story at the starting line. He has exposed and stopped many other accounts.

She asked me how she could talk to her people and have them believe my story. Well, instead I asked her to go to her people and ask them the same question I had given to her. "Ask them about Isaiah, and about the Psalms," I told her. "You know that I believe Jesus is your Messiah. Behind safe closed doors, deeply examine Scripture to see if Jesus might have fulfilled your own prophecies, because that's what first-century Jews did, and that's why so many of them became followers of Jesus. Because *he is* the Messiah."

My main goal was not that she or her readers would believe my story. Frankly, in the end the point was not about getting a glimpse of Heaven in the first place anyway. The point is that my son's experience confirmed who the God of Heaven is. Whether she believed my story or not, the story I wanted her to believe most was the story of Jesus Christ.

I remember the words of the same angel Gabriel who had appeared to the prophet Daniel in the Old Testament of Hebrew Scripture. He showed up to tell a young but faith-filled Hebrew teenager called Mary about the coming Christ in her. "Don't be afraid, Mary," the angel told her, "for you have found favor with God! You will conceive and give birth to a son, and you will name him Jesus. He will be very great and will be called the Son of the Most High. The Lord God will give him the throne of his ancestor David. And he will reign over Israel forever; his Kingdom will never end!"[10]

EVERYTHING THAT HAD HAPPENED

They killed Jesus on a Friday, nailed him to a cross, and hung him outside the city walls. At one time, thousands of people had followed him. Dozens were constantly there at his teachings. They weren't the inner circle of twelve disciples that Jesus had chosen, but they were hearing many of the same things. They were there when Jesus multiplied a boy's lunch to feed thousands. They saw him heal the blind and cast out demons. They heard him offer parables that were so easy to listen to, but at times difficult to understand. They saw him offer the kindest of smiles to orphans and widows and the sick, and the harshest of rebukes to prideful religious leaders and hypocritical manipulators of every station.

Two men were among this broader circle; they were disciples of Jesus, but not of "The Twelve," as they were called. After Jesus died, Cleopas and his friend had left Jerusalem on a road to the east, just as many other followers were quietly leaving the city at the time. The trip was going to take at least half a day, perhaps more depending on what they carried. Five to six hours is a long time to walk.

They were frustrated, scared, and confused. The story is recounted well in Luke 24. It says that as they walked the road, "they were talking about everything that had happened."[11]

Everything that had happened is a code phrase for those with a life-shattering experience. A plane crash takes out the parents of half a dozen kids, and everyone is terrified of what's next. The extended family gathers for a dual funeral and to discuss everything that had happened. A community is flooded, dozens lose their homes, neighbors and family members gather at a local high school to discuss everything that had happened. A single mother gets busted for drug possession, and then gets sentenced to fifteen years. The aunts and uncles gather the kids and discuss everything that had happened. An earthquake devastates a city. After a few days' digging through rubble for the lost, the city leaders, rescue personnel, and relief workers gather to discuss everything that had happened.

People "talk about everything that had happened" from that point on with a peculiar symbolic language, have you noticed? They say, "Yep, that was before November 1997." Or they say, "The winter Mom and Dad died." They might call it "the year from hell" or "the day it all blew up." They might give it names like "her emotional train wreck" or "the family earthquake" or "the community crisis" from then on.

THE WEEK FROM HELL

Cleopas and his friend hiked for half a day out of Jerusalem talking like this. They had believed Jesus. They knew him to be a prophet, a healer, and so much more. They had thought he might even be the Messiah. But then it all went to pot.

The week from hell came right before Passover. It ended with Jesus arrested and accused, a mob calling for his head, stoked by the high priests of their own religion. Jesus was crucified by the Romans. It was the darkest day they had ever known in the worst week of their lives.

However, that very morning as they were leaving town, they heard some weird reports. Some women had been to the tomb where they had laid Jesus, and it was empty. The huge stone the government had put there was rolled away, and the Roman guards were nowhere to be seen.

People were already speculating, some suggesting that Jesus had risen from the dead. More than a few worried that the authorities had come to take his body and might not treat it with due honor—robbing him of even that final dignity in this horrible week. Some wondered if a few rogue disciples had come to steal the body, trying to fabricate the story of his resurrection.

These two men walking out of Jerusalem were talking about all of this. They were debating it and taking sides, then switching sides and talking more. Their conversation swirled in circles.

They were so engrossed in their conversation that they didn't notice another man was walking just behind them, gaining on them silently, and in fact close enough when they noticed him to hear their conversation.

The stranger asked them, "What are you discussing so intently as you walk along?"[12]

Mildly embarrassed, they looked back at him with a short wave and were going to let him pass them. As they did so their faces fell. They were sad and discouraged.

Cleopas then wondered why this stranger didn't know right away what they must be talking about, since the man was certainly leaving on the Jerusalem road like them. "You must be the only person in Jerusalem who hasn't heard about all the things that have happened there the last few days," Cleopas mused.

"What things?" the stranger asked.

Cleopas and his friend recounted "all that had happened" in a few short sentences for this man who must have been living under a rock to have missed it.

They were talking about the hard stuff: "...the things that happened to Jesus, the man from Nazareth," they said. "He was a prophet who did powerful miracles, and he was a mighty teacher in the eyes of God and all the people. But our leading priests and other religious leaders handed him over to be condemned to death, and they crucified him. We had hoped he was the Messiah who had come to rescue Israel. This all happened three days ago."

They were also talking about the astonishing, unbelievable stuff. "Then some women from our group of his followers were at his tomb early this morning, and they came back with an amazing report. They said his body was missing, and they had seen angels who told them Jesus is alive! Some of our men ran out to see, and sure enough, his body was gone, just as the women had said."[13]

WALKING THROUGH SCRIPTURE

The stranger listened carefully to them recount the story, nodding at the appropriate moments. They were now a trio, walking with staffs up a sharp incline, perhaps approaching the halfway point of their trip.

But then the stranger took a more confrontational stance: "You find it so hard to believe all that the prophets wrote in the Scriptures. Wasn't it clearly predicted that the Messiah would have to suffer all these things before entering his glory?"

The stranger took them to the writings of Moses first, Genesis through Deuteronomy, and talked of the foreshadowing of the Messiah. Then he went on to the Psalms and the prophets. He pointed out the virgin birth prediction of Isaiah and Micah's Bethlehem prediction, both matching Jesus' birth. He reminded them that Jesus came out of Egypt just as Hosea said.[14] He mourned with them the massacre of Bethlehem at the birth of the Messiah and pointed out that he was not only from Nazareth, as the Scripture said, but also ministered in Galilee, just as Jeremiah and Isaiah predicted.[15]

He told them that they should be encouraged that Jesus was betrayed by Judas and mocked by the Roman guards, as these things fulfilled prophecies in Zechariah and the Psalms.[16] Yes, Jesus' hands and feet were pierced as he was crucified and people gambled to take his clothes, leaving him naked on the cross, but this was not something to cry about—it was something to rejoice about. This not only fulfilled Psalm 22 but also showed that he was crucified for their sins.[17]

The stranger knew Scripture well; he was clearly as knowledgeable as any Jewish rabbi. He walked through the entire Hebrew Bible on the road, showing Cleopas and his friend how this all came together just as God wanted, and that Jesus was indeed the Messiah.

A STRANGE STRANGER

They must have slowed their pace quite a bit to pay attention to this stranger, because the afternoon sun was low by the time they reached their destination, the city of Emmaus. As they approached the turn to their house, the stranger acted like the conversation was over, and he was going to keep traveling on. But Cleopas and his friend begged the man to spend the night with them, pointing to the sun now reaching the end of the day.

The stranger agreed and went into their home, where they prepared a meal. They asked the stranger to bless the meal, so he reached out and grabbed a piece of bread. He then broke it in half, and lifted it up to the width of his shoulders as he prayed to the Father, blessing their meal.

Cleopas might have been peeking a bit during the prayer, seeing that this moment had such an uncanny resemblance to the day he saw Jesus hold up bread before multiplying it for the thousands. The words he used to pray reminded him so much of the words of Jesus in his parables and stories. As the stranger said, "Amen," he reached out both halves of the bread, handing them to Cleopas and his friend. He looked at Cleopas with such kindness and love, and at that moment, it was as though a filter over his eyes was removed and Cleopas realized: *Jesus is handing me this bread.*

The stranger was the Savior. The stranger was the one talked about throughout Scripture. The stranger knew the verses so well not because he was just a brilliant rabbi—he knew them because he'd inspired them in the first place. The stranger wasn't just a stranger on the road, he was a stranger to this earth. He was the Messiah!

Just as this realization dawned on Cleopas and his friend, the stranger disappeared into thin air. The two men looked at each other with confused but elated expressions, wondering for a moment what to do next. Without a word, they gathered their things for a trip again and headed out the door, like children about to see a friend open a present they'd bought and wrapped themselves.

The sun was beginning to set on Emmaus by now. It would be a dark and dangerous trip back to Jerusalem to find the disciples and tell them what had happened—to confirm for them what they were doubting—that Jesus had indeed risen from the dead. They were excited not only to share that news, but also to march through the Scriptures in the way the stranger had shown them.

Cleopas, with a walking stick in one hand and a sack on the other shoulder, put his free arm around his friend and smiled. The friend said to him, "Didn't our hearts burn within us as he talked with us on the road and explained the Scriptures to us?"[18]

HEARTS BURNING WITHIN

Two thousand years later, in the Jerusalem that Cleopas and his friend were walking toward, an Israeli reporter was talking with me about Heaven and Jesus. I don't know if the message of Jesus burned in her heart. I don't know if she fully understood how her faith's prophecies were fulfilled in my Jesus. I'm sure I didn't explain it as well as the stranger did to Cleopas and his friend. But I did tell her, "I believe that God understands that people are affected by their culture or other religions. I think God wants you to know that he wants nothing more than to help you, and he loves you so much that he sent this Messiah first to your people. He still cares about you the same way. He's thinking about you and he wants you to know the answer to this question even more than you want to know it."

That same thing is true for you whether you're a Jew like this woman or not.

I hope that the prophecies of the one and only Messiah burn in her heart and others she might have spoken to that day.

Because I'm always as happy as a kid with a present to see someone open the gift of Jesus Christ.

Maybe like this reporter, you've never heard any of this before, either. It sounds like God had put a lot of thought into exactly how he was going to build his bridge to the entire world. No good architect or engineer would start to build anything without drawing up specific plans, blueprints, expense sheets—a complete picture. God, the greatest planner, didn't either. And he executed every detail just as he had planned.

10

MY GREATEST UNANSWERED PRAYER

Why does God seem to not answer some of my most important prayers?

Because the major motion picture adapted from our story was a huge box-office hit, we had to work very hard to keep some semblance of normalcy in our lives and to keep our children grounded. One thing in the middle of it all kept things very real for me, perhaps *too* real. My father was dying.

I had done over three hundred interviews about this movie in just a seventy-day span, and I was depleted. It always made me grin when our dog Princess would yawn so long and hard and clench her sleepy dog eyes and stick her tongue out when she was worn out. I was *that* kind of tired, the big-gaping-dog-mouth-yawn kind. I prefer the slower patterns of life back in Imperial, Nebraska. I'd rather my attention be on our spectacular red-and-orange sunsets and bright-golden sunrises, not clunky publicity calendars. And it feels far more real and important to respond to my fire alert beeper than to take a call from a reporter.

We planned several times of rest that year, but each one was interrupted by an emergency. I felt like a hamster on one of those endlessly spinning wheels. Just when I thought I could get off the hamster wheel, I got the call: My father's health was failing. They thought he could go "at any moment." We didn't have much time.

Have you ever had the phone ring and your first thought was about the sadness of the news, and your second thought was about how it would change everything you'd do for the next few weeks or months of your life? That was this call.

Perhaps you've been in a room like his in a nursing home with a heavy wide door opening to a small room. Most people who take up residence in such a place put up drawings from grandkids and pictures of family, but not my father. His room was very plain—as if he was just passing through, even though it had become his home. A few books leaned against the side of a bookshelf. A handful of pictures on a table seemed as lonely as the sole occupant. My dad apparently didn't have many things that were precious to him anymore. It was just a simple and plain place of pain.

I stood over his bed, watching him waste away, his body shrinking before my eyes. The sockets of his eyes got larger in proportion to his head. I could see the death cycle nearing the end.

It was close to 2 a.m. as I sat by his bed. He opened his eyes and tried to talk, but I couldn't understand him; the words came out as random noises. But he reached up to me. I asked him if he knew it was me, and he nodded yes. That was the last time he responded to me, but he kept hanging on, even without accepting food or drink. It was hard to watch, and sometimes I just had to look away.

The doctors said he could die at any moment, but the painful days and nights dragged on. I prayed that God would just take my dad and end the suffering. I was desperate. But God wouldn't answer that prayer for twelve days as my father wasted away without food, water, or an IV. I just didn't get it. I couldn't understand.

HOSPICE

I spent a good deal of time in that small room wrinkling my nose at the mixture of body odors and antiseptic smells that always permeates the air in places like this. A hospice nurse came in and began working with my dad. She was a little younger than me, with brown shoulder-length hair. She wore plain casual clothes and tan shoes with thick soles with no identifying logos. I imagine rushing around caring for others all day long requires a good pair of shoes.

I was so impressed with the care she gave my dad. When he could no longer drink liquids, she would sit gingerly on the edge of his bed and squeeze water down his throat with a syringe to relieve his thirst. She was so sensitive to helping with things I didn't even know needed to be done.

Sometimes his breaths would be thirty to forty seconds apart, and I was on edge with the waiting, thinking that perhaps this time would be his last. She told me that she had timed it, and sometimes he would go forty-five seconds, followed by a gasp for air. As a hospice nurse, she had of course seen all of this dozens of times before. She had walked through more valleys of death than I had ever seen.

I was physically and emotionally exhausted, at one of the worst moments of my life. I was shedding tears and praying out loud at times, and she was the only one to talk to in the middle of the night. We talked about the difficulty of watching a parent go through this. She shared some of her difficulties in life as well, which made her question God.

At one point during our conversation, I said, "I don't believe in accidents; I believe in appointments."

"Yeah, I know that's what you believe," she said.

I asked her how.

She pointed at a book on the shelf in the corner. "That's you. I read your book. The very beginning of that book says, 'I don't believe in accidents, I believe in appointments.' And that movie my teenager went to see, that was about you."

In that moment, when so many were flocking to see a movie about my family, this woman in the nursing home was seeing the difference between perception and reality. I suppose my angst in that room looked very different from the tone of the hopeful Heaven-focused experience people saw in the movie. But she was seeing the real me.

THE TEST

Once, at a book signing, I was approached by a woman who slapped down a picture of a sea creature. I looked down, then looked up at her face filled with emotions I couldn't quite discern. "Do you know where this was taken?" she asked.

"Well, that's a stingray in a petting tank. And from the surroundings in the picture I think it might be from the Butterfly Pavilion in Denver." We'd visited the Butterfly Pavilion as a family and talked about the experience in *Heaven Is for Real*.

I looked up at her and could see that a question was resolved in her mind. She nodded with a sense of reassurance. "That's what I needed to know."

I realized that she was testing me. The picture was an investigation to see if the stories we told in the book were made up.

"We went there the same year you did, to the same Butterfly Pavilion in Denver, with my little girl, who had an intestinal leak—very similar to the crisis your son faced," she told me. "We prayed just like you did for her to recover. But she died." The little redheaded boy standing in front of her finished the sentence: "I have to be the big brother now."

I looked into the heartbroken eyes of that boy who'd lost his sister. I wasn't sure if any answer would be enough in that moment. When my son was dying, I cried out to God in a little chapel in the hospital, and God answered that prayer. Dozens of people have contacted me with frustration in response to my son's experience. It was something I hadn't thought of at first. They wondered why God had answered my prayer and hadn't answered theirs.

How could I respond to that? Perhaps with what I said at my dad's funeral: "Here lies my greatest unanswered prayer."

THE FUNERAL

My dad did finally pass away, after suffering much longer than I prayed he would. And then I had to preach at the funeral.

Standing on stage is hard enough. Standing behind a pulpit makes it worse. But when that pulpit is above a casket holding your father's body, you choose your words wisely. You want to be sure you say the right thing.

I don't know if the words I chose were the right ones. But they were the ones that came to me: "Here lies my greatest unanswered prayer."

Few things are as difficult as working through the pain of losing a parent. It is even more complicated when your relationship with that parent is the source of many of your struggles in life.

When I was younger, my mother would send me off to live with my grandfather, Pop. At the time, my father was going through a mental breakdown. He was first hospitalized when my mother was pregnant with me, and over time his behavior became more irrational and at times confrontational. My mother and others have talked about my father as a real man of God, someone who read Scripture and treated people well. I didn't know that man.

Instead, I grew up with a very dysfunctional relationship with my dad. At first, I didn't understand what was going on. I just knew I got shipped off from Oklahoma City to my grandparents' farm. My dad was quiet mostly. He didn't interact with us a whole lot when I was young. I remember that my mom had to push him very hard to connect at all.

He didn't do anything until Mom would yell at him enough to engage.

My awareness grew as I got older. Dad's illness grew progressively worse. He started losing jobs. His hospital stays lengthened. Then Pop died when I was seven, so my visits to the farm ended.

My parents divorced when I was eighteen. That left me with a hard decision to make: I had to either take care of my father or head off to college to start my own life.

I went to college. But the troubles followed me there. As an adult, I tried to insulate my children from the difficult parts of my relationship with my dad. I wanted to make sure my dad's bizarre behavior didn't affect them. But they started to realize what the situation was like. On one occasion, we went to see my brother and dropped by to see my dad. Colby was about nine, and Colton was about thirteen. They picked up on some things and told me later they didn't know it was that bad.

One month, in what seemed to be an isolated moment of selflessness, Dad randomly sent a packet with birthday cards for my whole family, all at once. Mind you, our birthdays fall throughout the year, not all in the same month. But I guess it's the thought that counts, right?

My wife didn't read my card first, or she said she never would have let me see it. He had filled it full of harsh words of anger toward me. I was grateful for his words to the family, but as he expressed his love and admiration for them he told me how much I'd let him down. It felt so horrible to be reminded again that he saw me as a big disappointment. No matter how old you get—if your parents still don't believe in you, it's hard to get your relationship with your Heavenly Father in the right trusting mode. Because of his paranoia, my dad turned people against me at every turn throughout my adult life, even at the end at the nursing home.

FATHER IN HEAVEN

Like many people whose relationship with their dad is difficult, I found it initially hard to think of God as my Father. But Scripture describes him that way. Jesus said: "Which of you, if your son asks for bread, will give him a stone? Or if he asks for a fish, will give him a snake? If you, then, though you are evil, know how to give good gifts to your children, how much more will your Father in heaven give good gifts to those who ask him!"[1]

But that is the problem. Because of his mental illness, my father was exactly the kind of man who might choose stones or snakes in this example Jesus gave. One time, he showed up on my campus and let all the air out of my tires so I couldn't go to work on time! How could I trust the idea of this Father in Heaven if I couldn't even trust my flesh-and-blood father on earth?

But somehow I grew in my faith. Somehow God gave me gifts not only of grace but also for ministry. Somehow this mixed-up kid became a pastor. But that doesn't mean I had worked through this relationship with my dad. It just didn't make sense to me—and it came to a head when he got more and more sick.

Sometimes that happens. It's like a broken garbage disposal:

Only when it breaks and you have to stick your hand down in the sink do you remember all the nasty things you stuffed down there, because you have to get your hands dirty in it all over again. When my dad's health started to fail, I had to get my hands dirty all over again, down in the garbage disposal of my soul.

I prayed for years that God would heal my father. I prayed when I was a kid and figured out something was wrong. I prayed as a teenager—never feeling like I had a truly normal home like my friends. I wanted that deeply. I prayed as a young adult, especially when I had my own children. But nothing changed.

My prayers seemed to leave my lips only to fall on the floor, not even being heard by God. So, that's why when I presided at my father's funeral and waved down to the casket holding his body, I said, "Here lies my greatest unanswered prayer."

In fact, I had three unanswered prayers related to my dad: that he would be healed from mental illness; that he would beat the health challenges he faced as he aged; and that he would at least die quickly and not suffer in pain, making me watch the torture. God didn't answer any of these prayers the way I wanted him to.

The irony of my unanswered prayers at that funeral is that many people who'd read *Heaven Is for Real* at that moment were mad at me because many of my other prayers *were* answered. But let's get real. Many people pray just like I did, and many ask for just a small miracle. Just a little hope. And then they don't get it. And then they hear about a kid who experienced Heaven, and while they appreciate it, it makes them angry. I got multiple miracles and a whole lot of hope. They got nothing. That's how they see it.

Perhaps it is good for you to know that not all my prayers are answered like I want them to be. I prayed my dad would be healed of his mental illness and he wasn't. What's more, it was an unanswered prayer because I just couldn't understand the justice of it all. On the one hand, my father was horrible to me, and did things that no Christian should ever do. That behavior told me he didn't belong in Heaven. But I also was deeply troubled over the salvation of my dad. Others spoke of his faith in Christ and dedication as a young man before his illness, before it all started going downhill. Was that faithful man my real father, or was it the mixed-up one I experienced?

I struggled with what Jesus said before he left his own disciples: "Do not let your hearts be troubled. You believe in God; believe also in me. My Father's house has many rooms; if that were not so, would I have told you that I am going there to prepare a place for you?"[2]

Was there a room prepared for my dad? What if he lost it in his descent into partial madness?

Over the years, my real Father in Heaven began to give me more of his understanding. It was an experience with my father that actually helped me. As my dad aged, he got diabetes. His pancreas stopped producing the insulin he needed. This also affected his behavior in bad ways. This, perhaps, was a little easier for me to handle. I just chalked his crankiness up to his pancreas. God's understanding came to me: *Someone doesn't lose their salvation just because their pancreas stops working.*

So could I extend the same grace to his mental illness?

Dad doesn't lose his salvation just because his brain isn't working right. I needed that, because some of my dad's terrible behavior haunted me.

My prayer life went through a major shift.

I started changing my prayers. *God, I know who he was, and somewhere inside of him is that man of God. It's just that his brain isn't working right now. So I do believe he will be in Heaven.* Changing my prayer helped me work through that.

Instead of praying for God to heal his mental illness here on earth, I prayed for the future. *God, if you're not going to heal him down here—can I at least meet my real dad in Heaven? I never had that relationship with him here, but can I have that in Heaven?*

NEW UNDERSTANDING

God didn't answer my prayers for my dad's healing on earth. But I could sense God saying, "Yes, you'll have that. You'll have that relationship with your dad in Heaven."

During this, I heard stories that others were treated well by him in certain moments when he was in the nursing home. Glimpses of the man of God were in there. I could believe that inside him there was still a man who had read the Bible and made commitments to believe in Jesus Christ and follow him. When his brain and body were in his control, he was that man. When they weren't, he wasn't. I'm hanging on to the answer that one day God is going to give me that chance to meet my real dad.

And with it, I was able to release him. I could move on.

I think others deal with this, particularly when someone

they love slips into some kind of dementia. I knew a retired minister whose wife was so racked with horrible pain and a dozen illnesses that her entire demeanor changed. The once sweet and kind woman became a terror to be around. "She just isn't herself anymore," the kind old minister apologized.

A professional woman I know who's in her fifties had to take a full month of leave off work to care for her mother in a rotation with her siblings. Because her mother had Alzheimer's disease, this daughter said, "Not only does she not recognize me because of the disease, I honestly barely recognize *her* anymore because of how much she's changed."

In these situations, a loved one can become hateful and nasty. You start to wonder like I wondered: "Is there a room being prepared in Heaven for her?" "Lord, is he still the man he was, inside there?"

I'm here to say: Don't lose hope. Don't give up. You might not understand. But God does. He knows. Learn to "Trust in the Lord with all your heart and lean not on your own understanding."[3] He can give you the peace that Scripture speaks of, "which transcends all understanding."[4]

STILL ANGRY

The fact that I was coming to town to preach the message for my dad's funeral had caused a bit of a ruckus. The pastor of the church was receiving multiple complaints, as people were angry with me because my dad had said a bunch of awful things, made-up things, about me while at the nursing home. My reputation among most of the nursing home staff and residents was shot. They didn't think I should be allowed to speak at the funeral.

But I did share at the funeral, giving much of this story and my heartache in the process. After the service, the pastor said to me, "People are still angry, but for a different reason now: They are angry because they all want copies of the funeral message, because they know people who need to hear this. The problem is we don't normally record funeral messages so we don't have it on tape, and now they are angry at *me!*"

UNEXPECTED ANSWER TO PRAYER

The hospice nurse now saw me as a regular guy going through loss, something she sees all the time.

I didn't understand why God let my dad hang on in pain for so many weeks. Then after that funeral someone called my brother and told him that that very hospice nurse had decided to put her faith in Christ. Finally I understood: God wanted her to see me with my dad. He wanted my struggle and hurt to influence her in those awful moments to make a difference.

Over the last few years, I've come to realize that my greatest unanswered prayer was the place where God is giving me the greatest dose of his spiritual understanding. Isn't that how our real God works? He turns everything on its head, and in the end the stuff that makes no sense starts to make the most sense of all.

God was working even when I couldn't tell for sure if he was listening to my prayers. I don't understand why my father was allowed to go through that mental illness. I don't know why he treated me so badly because of it. I don't fully understand it—but God, through his grace, is giving me part of his spiritual understanding that goes beyond my own. And God doesn't promise us that we are going to understand everything. Maybe in Heaven I'll understand it more, or I won't need to understand it. I continue to have faith in the midst of what I don't understand.

In this case, God did show me why he answered my prayers in a different way than I asked for. And maybe, just maybe, just a little of the reason is in the words you're reading right now. Maybe he wanted you to understand a little more, too.

11

THE BIG DEAL OF THE CROSS

I 've seen shows and paintings of Jesus dying on a cross… it 's torture. Why is the cross so important to Christians?

There are two main ways to view the cross: either as a story, or as a symbol. As a symbol, a cross is a bit strange. When you think of what a cross is, then it is sort of like putting an electric chair at the front of a sanctuary, or wearing a gold lethal injection syringe around my neck, or getting a tattoo of a hangman's noose on my biceps. These are dark images but would be parallel because the cross is an instrument of death—and in many ways is worse than these other symbols, because the cross was intended for torture before death. In the days of Jesus, the lucky ones were beheaded—quick but painless. Crosses were meant to send a message to the masses: *If anyone thinks about repeating what these guys did, you are put on notice. You will die publicly, slowly, and with as much agony as possible.*

But for the follower of Jesus, a cross is not a symbol. It's not about ideas. It's about history. It's about *his story*, in fact.

That story, the story of the cross, is actually the story of more than one cross. Perhaps you've seen it before: not just a cross by itself, but three of them, with a taller middle one in the foreground. This is a hint at the story. It's a hint at a conversation that happened among the three people who hung on those crosses that helps us understand the meaning of the cross.

Two other criminals were hung to the left and right of Jesus. One berated Jesus, but the other said, "'We deserve to die for our crimes, but this man hasn't done anything wrong.' Then he said, 'Jesus, remember me when you come into your Kingdom.'"[1]

Jesus didn't miss a beat. Even in the middle of his pain he replied, "I assure you, today you will be with me in paradise."[2] That story is the key beyond the symbolism. The story *is* the meaning.

THE SIMPLE MEANING OF THE CROSS

The cross is a deep truth that is hard to fully grasp at times, but there are parts of it that are very simple to understand. As when we're solving a problem or building something, we shouldn't skip the simple, basic things—that's the place to start. The Bible is that way about the cross; it is a simple equation. I wonder if some of us would rather focus on the unclear stuff than the clear stuff. Christians and non-Christians both quickly focus on the complex disagreements instead of the simple things that can be agreed upon.

With the cross, we need to remember it's all about relationships.

My son Colton has a vivid memory of the relational nature of the cross. When experiencing Heaven, he noticed that no one there wore glasses or had any kinds of scars on their body. But when he got to Jesus, he saw the marks on his hands. He asked Jesus, "Why do you have those markers on you?" Jesus said, "It's to remind me how much I love you."

A CROSS OF RELATIONSHIP

We forget that one of the things that many of us could relate to about the cross is that this involves a father seeing his son die. Perhaps you've found images of Jesus dying, especially the really accurate depictions of the torture, disturbing. I know I've seen movies that offend people because they are so realistic about what happened. It's hard for you and me to watch. Think of how hard it was for God.

Some have said that God looked away from the cross, turned his head, or abandoned Jesus because God cannot look on sin. But God looks at sin all the time. If God can't look on sin, he can't look on you or me or any of the world. It's much more simple and relational than that. The Bible even says, "You spread out our sins before you—our secret sins—and you see them all."³ God didn't turn his back on the cross because he couldn't look at sin, he turned his back because he just couldn't look anymore upon his son.

I know how that feels. Perhaps you have a child or a relative you couldn't imagine watching go through pain. When I witnessed my son dying, the way his body was just suffering and jerking around, the agony he felt—that was painful for me to watch. Everything in me wanted to switch places with him. I couldn't do anything about it. The difference is that God *could* do something about it. God is all-powerful. So, he had to look away or he might have stopped it. God has experienced that tragedy personally. I wish it would break our heart more that we break God's heart.

Maybe you can't imagine God feeling pain, but Jesus had two parents—an earthly one and a divine one. You can see Mary looking up crying uncontrollably; you can hear her cries even now because you can relate to pain and loss. The few friends that had the faith to join her have their arms wrapped around her. John is promising to take care of her, but nobody can or ever could console her in that moment. She is in agony.

At that moment, what does Gabriel dare say to God? Are the angels crying out, "Holy, holy, holy"? Or is Heaven silent? Is it full of the muffled cries of saints and angels as God the Father cries, too? What does God crying even sound like? You know and I know that nobody could console Jesus' dad in Heaven any more than anyone could console his mother on earth. He is in agony, too.

My son Colton was ten years old when the book about his story came out. So, I felt he needed to read the book (a book that is mostly about him). He wasn't too excited about being forced to read a book written by his dad, so he tried to avoid it. Constantly busy, he just didn't have time because there was always a better option that would suddenly appear on his daily calendar. I had to force the issue. "Colton, school starts in about three weeks. You are going to have this book read by then, so you will read five chapters per day until you're done.

And once you start, don't you quit reading each section until you have finished all five chapters. Or else!"

Knowing that I was serious, Colton started. But he still waited until late in the day to get started, every day. The first evening went by as expected. The first five chapters are pretty short, but not necessarily any longer than any other set of five chapters. He took about forty-five minutes to dredge through them, constantly reminding himself that it was his best option at the time. On the second evening, however, he finished reading and was upstairs in the kitchen in less than twenty minutes. I was surprised, because I knew he couldn't have finished all five chapters that night as he had been explicitly told to do.

I walked into the kitchen and Colton was facing away from me, making a sandwich. I said, "Hey, Colton, you are supposed to be reading. I know you aren't a speed-reader. There is no way you've finished reading those five chapters already." But he didn't turn around; he just stood there. He finally turned around slowly, and he was crying. He couldn't talk. He walked over to the counter next to me with his face red. Before he could even start talking, he had to take a moment to compose himself.

"Dad, I had to stop. I just finished chapter eight." (That's the chapter called "Raging at God" where I broke down and yelled at God to not take my son.)

He continued, "I'm sorry, Dad. I just forgot how much all of this hurt you and Mom. I had to stop."

I didn't know what to say. I was now crying like him, and my face was red from pain, too. I just told him, "I know, son.

While you were enjoying Heaven, knowing that we could lose you was really hard on us down here."

Wow—this was the moment when he realized the deep hurt for us, not just for him.

That's the kind of emotions we who believe in the cross begin to have: We realize that our sin hurts God, and that he feels about that hurt the way we might feel about our own hurts. God hurt when his son died. Anyone who looks at a gold cross hanging from a lady's neck and thinks it's just a nice piece of jewelry has no idea that that piece of jewelry represents God's greatest pain.

A CROSS OF PAYMENT

In my human mind, I don't know why the cross was so necessary. I know it was predicted. When Abraham was tested about offering his son to God, it foreshadowed how severely God would be tested offering his son for us. Even though a substitute was found for Isaac, no substitute was found for Jesus. He is the substitute. You see, Abraham's offspring should have paid the price for his own rebellion. But God in his love made the most painful decision possible. He planned even then to give his son in exchange for us to make our lives new again and provide unfailing love. God never fails to keep his promises.

In fact, Jesus asked the same question while praying in the Garden of Gethsemane. Even Jesus was wondering if it was necessary, so I think it's okay for us to ask God this question. But the answer from the Father was that this was the plan. Jesus checked on it already—and yes, it was not "his will" but it was the "will of the Father."

Clearly sin is not okay. And something needed to be done about it. Jesus took our sin upon himself to solve the problem of sin—to provide a way to defeat sin and death and start a powerful revolution that changed all of history. He needed to walk through this valley to guide us up the glorious mountain on the other side.

The cross represents a story; it is bigger than symbolism. The kind of wood doesn't matter, the way the cross is formed doesn't matter. In fact, many traditions form the cross in different ways; some have interpreted the cross to look like an X or like a T. Some show a fancy cross, some a simple one. The reality is that the cross was just the *method* for how the son of God died. When we say "the cross" we don't mean that the actual *cross* was key. If Jesus was beheaded, as his prophet cousin John was, perhaps that would be immortalized like the Crucifixion. The point was to take on our sin, to die in our place, to provide a path to victory afterward, and to begin a revolution for all time.

There is a great passage in the Bible that helps us think through how to focus our attention on what matters about the cross, Hebrews 12: "Therefore, since we are surrounded by such a great cloud of witnesses, let us throw off everything that hinders and the sin that so easily entangles. And let us run with perseverance the race marked out for us, fixing our eyes on Jesus, the pioneer and perfector of faith. For the joy set before him he endured the cross, scorning its shame, and sat down at the right hand of the throne of God."[4]

Let's talk about the different parts of these verses.

CLOUD OF WITNESSES

This metaphor, a "cloud of witnesses," is just the idea of a bunch of people who went before us being able to see what is happening (they witness the events of today). This is a beautiful way to start our conversation about the cross.

The reality is that our loved ones see us from Heaven. The grandmother who likely prayed for you? She can see you from Heaven. That friend who passed on in the prime of life? He is a witness, too.

What's more, all the heroes of the faith mentioned in Hebrews 11 are watching, too. These known and unknown faithful ones are a witness to our encounter with the cross today.

HINDERS AND ENTANGLES

We've talked about sin and temptation a few times in these pages. Some things aren't sin but can still hinder or entangle you: neutral but difficult circumstances, or maybe even the good things that become a distraction. It might be an experience you had with a religious leader. It might be a childhood trauma, or a recent relationship. To come directly to Jesus on the cross, we must throw off these things that hinder and entangle.

This is part of why this book is written in the way it is. I want to write in a way that is simple and tangible for you as a reader, something that makes sense to regular people like you and me. You don't need a master's degree to understand and receive the grace of God. Whatever might stop you or trip you up on your way to a clear look at the cross, throw it off just as the above passage says.

RUN WITH PERSEVERANCE

My wrestling coach in high school would send us on a four-mile run *after* practice. Running has always seemed like torture to me, not exercise. Honestly, I still hate it. I have bad foot arches, and my age reminds me of the ankle I broke long ago that makes it especially hard for me to run.

Are you a runner? Do you like persevering when you run? Does it seem like it's worth it? Though I don't think running is worth it, in spiritual things I do persevere because it *is* worth it. I can keep in shape in ways other than running, but I can't keep in spiritual shape without engaging God directly. I have to listen to him and focus on Jesus and the Bible, which tells me about God.

FIX YOUR EYES ON JESUS

Let me tell you a new experience for me. I felt like God led me to learn Spanish. This is good because I now work with several people who speak only Spanish.

Here in Imperial, Nebraska, there is a potato processing farm where we do the bagging and shipping. I do mechanical work there one day a week, fixing things and doing some maintenance. There are usually about fifty to eighty employees there, and if something breaks down, there could be fifty people waiting to work, and trucks waiting to load up. So, we work on keeping equipment in top shape. Most of my work is on non-emergency fixes.

As I've worked there, I've noticed that about two out of every three of my co-workers are Spanish speakers. Almost a third of our small town's population is Hispanic.

I bring this up because my first language is English, so it's easy for me to speak in that language. I was born into an English-speaking family. It's my fallback point, my heart language. My history and background affect how I approach God.

I was taught to read the Bible, which is my spiritual core, my first language—in approaching God I always read the Bible then think about how God is speaking to me. But that doesn't mean I don't stretch myself in other directions.

The key is to fall back on the core practices that help you fix your eyes on Jesus, but also stretch you in new ways that help you focus, too. For instance, I've stretched myself to journal to gain more focus on God. I'm a pretty manly fella, and I used to think of journaling as a feminine thing, like a diary or something (not that it's a bad thing, I just didn't think it was for me). But I've journaled consistently now for about fifteen years. Now when I read the Bible, I journal afterward to apply the Word, rather than just thinking thoughts in my head.

A spiritual practice that is most stretching for me is to sit down and simply listen to God. That's not my heart language at all; it's like spiritual Spanish for my whole being. I don't like sitting down and just listening. I have to stretch myself to even pray through a list of requests. While I'm sitting in a room quietly, trying to let God talk, the silence is the hardest part. I feel like saying, *I'm waiting, God. I don't have a lot of time here, so speak up.* But when I do, I find that he has powerful things to say, things I'm so glad I took the time to listen for!

What are some ways that could help you fix your eyes on Jesus? Stretch yourself and start putting them into practice.

ENDURED THE CROSS

When you think of the fact that Jesus asked that the cup be taken from him in the Garden of Gethsemane, what does that tell you about this Jesus who still endured the cross for your sake? Why did Jesus ask if there could be another way? Jesus had thoughts just like you would in that situation. He knew it was the will of the Father, but he still asked.

Remember, this Jesus is the same person who said, "If you pray anything in my name you'll receive it," but he didn't get the answer he asked for. The cup wasn't taken from him. He wanted a different way—but he accepted the Father's plan. In his divinity, Jesus knew *why* this must happen, but his humanity felt the pain of the *how*.

We wonder if we can trust God, and if there might be another way than Jesus, and if there are other paths to Christ. Even Jesus asked the Father if there could be another way. He didn't want to have to go through the torture of the cross, and he asked that the cup representing that pain be taken from him so he wouldn't have to drink it. The answer was no.

I don't know all the ways Jesus finds people to save them, but I know that for the joy set before him, Jesus endured that cross for you and for me.

RIGHT HAND OF THE FATHER

What does it mean that Jesus is at the "right hand of God the Father"? It means that Jesus is the most important human in history. The glory of the son is accomplished, and the cross leads to the throne of God.

When we reject this cross, this son of God, we reject the Father, too. Think of the parent of a soldier who lays down his life for others. As a parent, you wouldn't be able to handle it well if anyone disrespected that sacrifice. You never want that sacrifice delegitimized.

In our humanity, we forget that God thinks that way about his son. I still wonder what would have happened if Jesus didn't say, "God, forgive them, they do not know what they are doing" while on that cross. I think that is the most important thing for us. We would have been toast. But Jesus gave us redemption.

That is the simple meaning of the cross. And so we can start there, kneeling at the foot of the cross. We can do that because the cross is not just a symbol. It is a true story. We can kneel before that cross because another person hung next to the cross and heard the amazingly good news before anyone else. The core story of the cross is that something happened there that made it possible for Jesus to extend grace to that criminal who "deserved to die," in his own words. Something happened there on the cross that made it possible to admit our own guilt, and ask Jesus to remember us when he comes into his Kingdom, and he said he would.

But there is still one more cross. If we don't talk about that one for a bit, we stop short of all the truth that comes with the cross.

THE WORST CROSS

Jesus died on a cross that had been prepared for a man named Barabbas. Due to Pilate's custom of releasing just one deserving criminal a year for public relations purposes, Barabbas lived and Jesus died in his place. Pilate declared Jesus innocent but caved to the crowds. World leaders do the same today. That's why public opinion can be the worst place to search for integrity or truth or justice.

The two criminals who died beside Jesus had to hate that decision. One criminal's rage was obvious. Hanging just as close to the thief who asked for Jesus' help was this man. He wasn't about to admit the wrongs he'd committed. He wasn't going to stand up for Jesus; he just went along mocking Jesus like the others. If God was going to let such an unfair thing happen between him and Barabbas, he wasn't going to go to his grave happy about it. He was blinded by his bitterness.

We don't know what the criminal on the other cross had heard about Jesus. Did he hear the crowds chanting outside the window to his cell? Could he have heard Pilate's pronouncement of Jesus' innocence? Did he see Barabbas smile, with arms held high and crowds cheering, as he walked to freedom? Had he at some time been a member of a crowd in more pleasant times, those times when people sat at Jesus' feet and listened to Jesus teach? Had he been one of the listeners, or had others told him about what they had heard Jesus say?

We don't know any of this for sure, but we do know he had time to think about his life and his destiny. He knew his sentence of death was certain. He probably spent much of that time hoping and praying that God would somehow have mercy on him on the other side of death.

At the hill beside Jesus, did he see the thorns smashed onto Jesus' head? Did he read the sign posted above Jesus, KING OF THE JEWS, before that cross was raised from the ground? Did he see the tears streaming down Jesus' face? We don't know, but we know he heard everything that was being said about Jesus, especially coming from his cohort hanging on the opposite side. Then he made a decision.

In his last few sentences spoken in this world, he stood up for Jesus. Something inside him helped him decide that Jesus was truly innocent. Jesus didn't belong where Barabbas belonged. Jesus was being treated more unfairly than he was. This man admitted that even though he was dying, there was no denying that he deserved his sentence.

He asked the other criminal, "Don't you fear God at all?" He knew he needed mercy. How could this other criminal not figure out that simple truth? Then turning to Jesus he prayed one of the most incomplete prayers the world has ever heard, but he put his hope and his faith in the only one who could give him mercy. And he received mercy.

The other criminal received—well, according to Scripture he received nothing. After Jesus promised this one humble, honest, and repentant criminal life, he never said another word to the other criminal mocking him from his other side.

Both criminals received just what they chose to receive. One wanted to reject Jesus, mock Jesus, shake his fist at God for a just sentence against his own crimes, and step into his eternity mad and upset with God. He got what he wanted.

The other asked for mercy from God. He didn't want to fight God. He wanted peace with God. Making a decision to stand for the one dying on that cross gave him the peace and mercy that he chose.

Jesus chose to die for all of us so all could make the choice to be forgiven. God gave to him what he chose as well.

Each person who died on that hill received what they chose.

12

THRIVING OR DYING

I go to church, but why isn't it working for me?

Like all parents, Nick and Kristi approached the arrival of their child with a great deal of expectation and not a little bit of fear.[1] You know it's going to be so great to have a little bundle of joy and smiles (not to mention dirty diapers and tears), but you also worry about how it will all happen. Every ultrasound was a time of anticipation mixed with "I sure hope..." and "Let's make sure..."

Little Cruz arrived just as any parent hopes, with ten fingers and toes, and all organs working fine. Before they knew it, they got out of the hospital and started being a family. He gained some weight, making it to about thirteen pounds. Then it happened.

Nothing.

It wasn't that *something* was wrong, it's that *nothing* changed. He stopped growing. For a while this didn't matter. Some kids go into a growth slump, and then later they have a growth spurt. The problem with Cruz was that he never hit the spurt. He just stayed thirteen pounds, constantly. Other things progressed, but he stayed very tiny and frail.

The tests began. Every arm or leg had needle marks. This thirteen-pound kid got hooked up to about every kind of strange machine you could imagine. Every kind of high-tech fluid or low-tech method was used to try to deduce what was up. Every test brought a new mix of emotions: They needed to know what was wrong, but didn't wish for the kinds of things being tested for to be true.

Finally, the specialists provided a diagnosis. It's not the kind parents would ever want to get. It's the kind of diagnosis that has no silver-bullet treatment and certainly no miracle cure. What was worse is that the specificity of the bad news was still coupled with a very vague disease. They said that Cruz had renal tubular acidosis—in lay terms, their son had a "failure to thrive." His body wasn't digesting food correctly, and he wasn't growing.

They were told the very harsh news that this was life threatening, and his prognosis would continue to be uncertain. What worse words could a parent ever hear?

Nick and Kristi went to the people of their church, my church, and several other churches completely broken by this news—but asking for all of us to somehow still pray. Our church has groups of people that pray in living rooms with pie and tea at night, in crowded church hallways on Sundays, and in small classrooms with bad coffee early in the morning. The hospitals and doctors had finished their work of prognosis and assessments, so the saints and sinners (and some who are a mixture of both) in my church and many other churches got to the task we know well and we know works: prayer with fasting.

But it was hard to have faith. We've heard many a bad prognosis in the past, only to see it cut short someone's future. We've prayed before and didn't get the results we hoped for, but we still do the work of prayer because we have seen it work miraculously, too. Even those with little faith will pray in a crisis. Nothing turns an agnostic into a prayer warrior like desperation. God doesn't always give the answers you thought you were praying for, but he always goes to work.

UNDENIABLE FAITH

It is important to know your stuff about what you believe. I don't want to discourage you from reading the Bible, or seeking hard answers to tough questions—much of this book is about those answers. However, in the end I don't want you to work hard giving an apology for your faith without also actively living your faith out. Defending your faith without living out your faith is all talk and no walk.

Perhaps you have a "failure to thrive" spiritually. Could it be that you're stuck with a thirteen-pound faith in a full-grown body, and you're having trouble digesting the spiritual stuff you hear and read? I would challenge you to live more dangerously. Most Christians choose to live by *safe* instead of by *faith*. If something is difficult or makes us feel uneasy, we have a tendency to back away from what God asks of us.

God responds to obedience more than anything else I have ever watched in people's lives. Christians get excited about their faith journey when they use some faith instead of just talking about the idea of it. God leads us when we pray, when we share our lives with others, or when we read from Scripture. He leads us through impressions of joy, by bumps of compassion, or even in moments of conviction. When we say yes to these leadings, God goes to work and we come out of our spiritual hibernation.

The two most excited people in my church right now did just that. Nate is a good friend, dependable, solid, but very quiet. You don't see him say many words unless he has a chance to torment my wife, Sonja. I kind of like that about Nate. But this last year, God started to torment Nate to leave his job, leave town, and plant pineapples in Sierra Leone. Yes, that's the country in Africa that just experienced the Ebola outbreak. This is the same country that God is trying to rebuild on the other side of the world. People need jobs. Devastated families need hope.

His wife, Cindy, had never flown out of the country before. After all the shots, after all the arrangements, and after all of the prayers, the trip from Nebraska to Africa began. There, Nate and Cindy helped local residents begin a pineapple farm, working with their hands. After two months, five acres were completed. Impressed by the progress and impressed by God, Dole now wants to grow those five acres up to forty acres. When Nate and Cindy returned to our church family, they had loads of stories to tell of how God kept "showing up on their journey of faith." Each yes led to more faith and to more energy and to more excitement.

Do you have to take a trip like this to see God bump

your spiritual life into a higher gear? I don't believe so. But I know you have to stop saying no and start saying yes to God. Toddlers seem to learn *no* as one of the first words of their vocabulary; it usually comes right after the word *Mom*, and unfortunately before the word *Dad*. Proudly and defiantly, our little ones begin their proclamations of self-determination long before puberty.

If God tells you to give an offering, and you say yes, you'll start growing. If God leans on you to serve, even serving middle schoolers in the youth group, and you say yes, you'll start stretching. If God asks you to listen to another's story and hurt, and you do, you will see both your compassion and your prayers increase. When God's spirit asks you to make reconciliation with someone you have wronged, and you say yes, you will begin to rewrite years of bad habits and careless words. You'll start intentionally building others up rather than callously tearing them down.

When someone says thank you for letting God use you in his or her life, it will be priceless. You will feel God's smile and you will be well on your way to thriving.

It's not enough just to be normal as a Christian. In fact, *normal Christian* is a bit of an oxymoron. We're supposed to be *abnormal*. We should be bouncing off the walls for Jesus. If we don't grow and progress, it can become life threatening. Your faith shouldn't stay in the same place like Cruz's weight did. The prognosis will eventually be similar: failure to thrive leading to a dying faith.

Also, don't compare yourself with someone else who isn't growing. As a pastor, I can't count the number of times I've heard someone compare themselves with a relative or co-worker just to let themselves off the hook. "At least I'm not like my sister, Lisa." Or, "I can count myself lucky that I'm further along than Jeff at work." Sometimes I think the prayer requests we give are just about other people whose lives are more screwed up than ours, so we can feel better about ourselves.

Don't seek good advice from those with bad character. Sometimes this means people who have sat in church for ages but never seem to enjoy God or their faith. They have had a lot of practice explaining away the "nos" of their life. The advice may seem wise, but it is tainted by their experience. You can't expect good words from a self-deceiving tongue. You can't expect good fruit from a bad tree. This isn't my opinion. Jesus said. "No good tree bears bad fruit, nor does a bad tree bear good fruit."[2]

There are only two things I get to take with me into the next life: my relationships, and my character. As Martin Luther said, "I have held many things in my hand and I've lost them all, but that which I have committed to God, I still have."[3] My relationships are the people who go with me, and my character is how I have responded and grown through my experiences. Find people whose character is worth following—their advice is what you want to listen to.

A THRIVING CHURCH

We often have frustrations with our church dynamics. The reason we are frustrated is that we all have in our gut an expectation that church life will model a thriving relationship, but all too often the church has a failure to thrive just like little Cruz did. Relationships don't grow, with each other or God, and that disappoints us.

But what if the church actually got it right?

There are two main illustrations the Bible uses to talk about the people of God. The first is "the children of God," and the second is "the Bride of Christ." Both are family relationships of health, protection, and devotion. Are there bad family examples out there? Yes. I lived in one. But that doesn't mean the ideal of a thriving family isn't worth fighting for.

The same is true for the church. Are there bad church examples out there? You bet. But that doesn't mean the ideal of a thriving church isn't worth fighting for. Thriving and growing church relationships are a minor miracle in the world today; when people see such relationships, they find them attractive. It shows an undeniable faith. When a church is in right relationship with God, it is a beautiful thing.

When a church isn't growing spiritually, it isn't thriving. And when something isn't thriving, it eventually is dying. The book of Hebrews counsels us this way: "And let us consider how we may spur one another on toward love and good deeds."[4] I've at times wondered if the Churchians out there would rather be a burr in the saddle toward anger than a spur in relationship toward love.

I will confess it: I haven't had a lot of super-impressive role models. So many I have looked up to have let me down. Perhaps I'm cynical, or maybe this happens to us all. Many people seem great till you get to know them well.

But one man has continually impressed me, even as I've gotten to know him better in his family and church relationships. The closer I get to him, the more I see his influence in people's lives like mine. Phil was my "boss" in the church. He was both my mentor and the man in authority over me. But if you asked him, he would just tell you that he was my friend.

Different leaders have different styles. But Phil had something a good deal too many church leaders don't have: His family seemed to enjoy him.

I know men who impress up front on the platform, but you can sense the disrespect and resentment coming from their homes. Sunday school teachers can tell you more about everybody in the church than anyone else. Kids let it all hang out, don't they?

Phil's kids are grown with spouses and children of their own. Both of Phil's grown kids do what I want my growing kids to do one day. They still hang out with their dad even though thousands of miles and dozens of states separate them from each other.

Phil's son is a major in the US Marines. He's a bit younger than me, but he's well traveled and impressively capable. Only the best of the best helicopter pilots get the opportunity to be on a crew entrusted to fly Marine One. I joke with him by calling him an overrated chauffeur, but there is no joking about it in truth. Phil's son can do things that most of us would dream about.

Yet year after year, this son takes time off to enjoy a vacation or hunt with his dad. Wow! How do you build the kind of lasting relationship with a child that when he is in his forties, he is still drawn to hang out with his dad? I didn't know, but I wanted to learn. So, I chose to get closer to Phil. I wanted to be close enough to model his habits and learn his lessons, so I might repeat the outcome I wanted to see realized in my own life.

Of course I've learned other things from Phil along the way. Phil knows how to resolve conflict. The church is one place to really refine this skill. Phil plainly but gently challenges people by asking them if they are happy with being part of the problem or if they'd be better off as part of the solution. His patience and his character help people trust him as he lets God use him to lead people and churches out of their messes.

Another of Phil's secrets is humility. He doesn't seem to take many things personally, nor does he ever waste hot air on filling his ego balloon. He legitimately remembers everyone's names, too—his brain is like a computer full of information about people. He prays for them and consistently greets everyone with the title he has given to me, "friend." Unlike me, everything about him is disarming to others.

I think God had a whole lot of reasons for putting Phil in my life. How else would a scrappy, independent, perfectionist wrestling coach like me learn real pastoral skills and attitudes?

The most important lesson I've learned from Phil still remains. It's a prayer he taught me that has transformed my life: "God, I don't care what people think of me today, but I care about what they think of your son because of me today. Amen." That prayer has changed everything. Maybe it will do the same for you.

THE UNDENIABLE

We kept on praying and praying for little Cruz who had failure to thrive. It was difficult to ask and not see an answer, but we kept giving God room to move while we prayed. Our prayers had the same motive as the one Phil taught me: Even if people thought less of us because our prayers seemed unanswered, in the end we cared what people thought about Jesus because of us, and because of little Cruz.

One day after hundreds had been praying for them, Nick and Kristi were in the waiting room in the children's hospital after a day of testing. A doctor came out to them and said, "I don't know what to say, but all of his tests are now normal. We cannot find anything wrong with him!" They praised God for this amazing news, astonished at the answer to all the prayers.

Because of his condition, Cruz still could not stand on his own at that point. After the doctor told them the miraculous news in the waiting room, they went to the desk to check out, just as any of us would. As they were doing so, Cruz stood up for the first time, right there on his own. It was as if God was confirming the miracle right before their eyes.

The other day I saw Cruz. I was struck with how articulate he is. He can form great sentences for his age. I loved seeing his energy, too. He was bouncing off the walls—a totally normal two-year-old, and I even wondered if he might be a bit *too* energetic. Cruz survived. No. Now that I think of it, he *thrived*. He's what they call a walking miracle. Although I myself like to think of Cruz as a bouncing-off-the-walls miracle.

When God shows up, our faith is explained in a way no argument or book or reasoned plea ever could. I often say that I don't just want a faith that's *defensible*, I want a faith that's *undeniable*. When I see little Cruz bouncing off the walls because of the prayer warriors who went to God for an answer, I see another example of the undeniable power God has to change lives.

But God doesn't just have the power to move stunted bodies from stagnation to growth. He has the power to move stunted faiths, too!

13

TINY KINGDOMS

Can God and politics be mixed?

Where I live in the far southwest corner of Nebraska, you're never far from farmers. Our entire economy and way of life are influenced not only by our farming past, but also our farming present and future. As I write this, it is harvesttime.

If you're not familiar with farmers, I should bring you up to speed. In most occupations, you need to be good at a handful of skills, but a farmer needs to be good at dozens of skills, a jack of all trades, fulfilling many different part-time roles: accountant, mechanic, businessman, agronomist, gardener, salesman, strategic planner, investor, and weatherman. Farmers must be good at all these things just to *survive*.

The potato farmer I work for has over eighty people working for him during harvest. The farmer must think like a king because of the scope of the decisions he or she makes. The equipment he or she buys, services, and repairs is sometimes more expensive and complicated than a Maserati.

One time, my phone rang on a Saturday morning at six fifteen. Now, Saturdays are a rare day that I get to sleep in. Like many bi-vocational pastors, my office number is my house number, so I was irritated that to be getting this call so early. I was kinda groggy, not completely awake, and there was a farmer calling me. He wanted me to drive two and a half hours to a site in another state that morning to meet him, and he wanted me to leave *right then*. The fact that I had to meet with other people that morning and had to finish preparing my sermon didn't matter to him at all. To say that he was bossing me around doesn't even begin to describe how he was acting. It was like he was a king and I was his subject taking orders.

As irritating as this was, farmers come by this kingly attitude honestly. They rule their land, so they end up thinking like kings. Many things can go wrong, so they must control what they can. Rain, drought, hail, storms, commodity prices, seed problems, fertilizer problems, pests, bugs, disease, regulations—most of these are out of their control. So, a farmer stands on twenty different teeter-totters at the same time, trying to find a balance among all the competing out-of-control factors.

Like kings, farmers are competitive. Farmers compare their kingdom with other kingdoms. If their row of corn isn't as straight as the other guys', they notice, and if theirs is straighter, they bring it up. Red and green mean a lot, too (John Deere or Case), and they give the other kings grief if they chose a different team. They don't shy away from jabbing each other at the coffee shop at dawn. They track who gets their planting in, or who gets it harvested first and best. In my town, the farmer who gets his harvest in first gets his picture taken and printed in the paper. Farmers will brag and compare their bushels per acre with each other as well. Just as farmers count bushels, rulers in all times count taxes. Which brings us to the Roman kings called Caesars.

RENDER UNTO CAESAR

When they couldn't pin down the infamous mobster Al Capone with any crimes, they just followed the money. And with some accounting investigation, they were able to prove a crime that took down the most notorious gangster of all time: tax evasion. There's a reason they say that nothing is certain but death and taxes. That's how powerful taxes are: They even took down Capone.

If you get a letter in the mail from the Internal Revenue Service, I bet you open that letter with a bit of fear. It could be good news, but more likely than not, it's not welcome news. It could be an audit. I've been audited, and I can tell you I'd rather go through almost any medical procedure than an audit. If an auditor starts demanding certain pieces of paper and you have filing cabinets full of papers from years past, you have to dig through those for the right receipt. The power that IRS agent has is very big: He or she can demand all kinds of things and fine you, not to mention potentially bringing charges.

Thousands of years before Al Capone, some religious leaders wanted to test Jesus and "trap him in his words," so they figured they'd try the question of taxes.[1] They asked him, "Teacher, we know that you are a man of integrity and that you teach the way of God in accordance with the truth. You aren't swayed by others, because you pay no attention to who they are. Tell us then, what is your opinion? Is it right to pay the imperial tax to Caesar or not?"

The reason this was a trap was because either way Jesus answered would get him in trouble. If he said no, don't pay taxes, then he could be reported to the Roman government as inciting people to defy Caesar (the king or emperor of the Roman world). If he said yes, do pay taxes, then people would be angry that he was going along with the evil and wicked Roman Empire that constantly infringed upon their Jewish rights.

Jesus saw right through it and said, "You hypocrites, why are you trying to trap me?"

Refusing to be caught, he raised the debate to another level. He said, "Show me the coin used for paying the tax." They handed him a denarius, which was worth about a day's wages.

Jesus asked them, "Whose image is this? And whose inscription?"

It was an odd question. Everyone knew whose face was on the denarius, just as you know that Abe Lincoln is on a penny, George Washington on a quarter, and Benjamin Franklin on a hundred-dollar bill. But Jesus asked the obvious question because he wanted them to give the obvious answer to make a point. I imagine he might even have been smirking at this point. The tables were turned.

"Caesar's," the people replied.

Jesus' next line has become somewhat famous: "So give back to Caesar what is Caesar's, and to God what is God's." In the King James Version, it says, "Render therefore unto Caesar the things which are Caesar's; and unto God the things that are God's."

What did this mean? Jesus was careful here not to fall into either of two traps, which are both traps for us today as well: He didn't fall into the trap of two wrongs making a right, nor did he fall into the trap of dependence on the culture around us.

SEEK PEACE AND PROSPERITY IN EXILE

Jesus was telling the people: Yes, you should pay your taxes. Why? Why would Jesus tell them to support one of the most bloody and unholy empires in history? The Jewish people lived under the thumb of their sacrilegious Roman overlord, who worshipped pagan gods and forced people to worship their Caesar like a god. If you think your president or prime minister is bad, he or she is nothing like a Roman emperor.

Emperor Caligula is known for his sexual deviance: He started a working brothel in his palace, committed frequent incest, and raped women at will (and then reported on the experience to the spouses of those he violated).

Emperor Nero was violent beyond belief, killing Christians and then blaming them for the burning of Rome. He even murdered his wife and mother.

Emperor Domitian was a paranoid conspiracy theorist, developed new ways to torture Jews, philosophers, and Christians, and was known to have impregnated his niece. He then forced her to have an abortion, and she died as a result.

Suddenly your head of state seems a little tamer in comparison, am I right?

So, why would Jesus tell us to pay taxes to this government? Some Jewish leaders preferred to stoke the fires of insurrection. But Jesus told them to submit to the taxes they needed to pay.

What's happening here is just following in the footsteps of a people who were used to exile. The Jewish people had been carried off into exile in Babylon for hundreds of years, and as they went, God gave them a command: "Seek the peace and prosperity of the city to which I have carried you into exile. Pray to the Lord for it, because if it prospers, you too will prosper."[2]

Jesus told them to obey their rulers, pay their taxes, and give authority to the lesser kingdoms of the world: giving to Caesar what is Caesar's. He knew that his Kingdom currency mattered most in the end, but in the meantime there was a measure of peace and prosperity that the kingdoms of this world could provide. As bad as Roman rule was, it was better than many alternatives of the day—the era was called the Pax Romana (Roman peace) for a reason. Sometimes when there is a big enough bully in charge, it drives every other bully underground.

Jesus doesn't fall into the trap of insurrection. Two wrongs would not make a right. So, when the government isn't what it should be, Jesus says: Yep, still pay your taxes.

CAESAR ISN'T THE REAL LORD

The second point Jesus made was about the "other side of the coin," literally. The people were thinking taxes, and instead he asked about the "carved image" on the coin. He also subtly reminded everyone that they are made in the image of God—

and what is valuable is the currency of humanity around them. He suggested that they are God's, but this silly coin is Caesar's. And what God has is lasting. We know this.

Jesus also subtly reminded them that the denarius itself was a direct violation of the second of the Ten Commandments. They are those same commandments that hang in courtrooms and city municipalities today, ever the target of any group that despises the integrity and justice that God asks of his people and of his leaders. That commandment is a rule about not using images intended for worship. By using this currency and becoming dependent on the culture around them, the religious leaders had themselves lost their focus on the true purity of their religion. Their dependence on God had been replaced by their new relationship with Caesar.

You don't have a denarius in your pocket right now, and none in the bank. You must go to an archaeological dig or a museum to find one. In fact, when another Caesar came along, he would carve his face into the coin and get rid of the old one. The currency of worldly kingdoms passes away, as anyone with an Ottoman Empire lira or Confederate dollar knows.

The coin Jesus held had Caesar's face carved on it in profile. On the back side, it had an inscription reading CAESAR IS LORD. Jesus was also pointing out that these Jews, who were trying to trap him, had become complicit in a government that worshipped a mere man. While Jesus didn't fall into the earlier trap of encouraging insurrection, he also didn't let his listeners off the hook for being so caught up in the Roman regime that they lost their distinctiveness.

These very men asking for spiritual guidance were the same

ones who were already making plans to use bribery, to recruit false witnesses, to spread fake news, and to build a mob that would march in the streets of Jerusalem to threaten the Roman governor Pilate. These men were not only aware of the loopholes and corruption of Caesar's government—they knew how to take advantage of all of it. They were just as corrupt in every way. Their actions demonstrated which kingdom their allegiance had shifted to.

In just a couple of days, these men would ask the Roman governor if he was a true friend of Caesar or not. On this day, Jesus pointed out that despite all of the religious dress and pretending, the lives of these religious leaders were a farce. Were they true worshippers of God?

FARMERS AND PHARISEES

Today far too many people do the same thing. They brush off their Sunday clothes. They press their shirts and pants. They comb their children's hair and head off to church. But just as soon as those clothes are put back into their closets, their obligation to God has been fully met in their minds. It's now back to the life they want to live.

Taking God home with you is the scary part and the sign of true devotion. He might ask you to be more caring to your spouse. He could bring up being a better example to your kids. He might even harass you about reading Bible stories to your children at bedtime. With God around, you might even be asked to censor your language, your entertainment, or your computer. It's just a whole lot easier to listen to God for the half-hour sermon than to change the unconfined life we live every minute at home.

Who is your lord? I believe it's the one children would say they see Mom and Dad follow at home. And as usual, they would be right on target.

We have aspirations, things we gotta get done. We have obligations to keep and stuff to buy. Much like farmers, we all have our own kingdoms to build. Does God give us the advantage today, or does Caesar give us the advantage? Like referees before a football game, someone has to toss a coin to see who gets the ball and who has to play defense. Most people can't even tell you which end of the field they will be playing on until the coin hits the ground. But they can play it either way. They have plenty of experience playing both sides of the ball—God's and Caesar's.

OTHER SCENES

This coin toss is replayed throughout Scripture. As followers of Jesus, we can render unto Caesar when appropriate, but we save and spend a different Kingdom currency. When King Jehoshaphat's enemies surrounded him, he knew that in the end it was not his kingdom or the kingdom that was attacking him that mattered: "Our God, will you not judge them? For we have no power to face this vast army that is attacking us. We do not know what to do, but our eyes are on you."[3]

Another story: Even though Shadrach, Meshach, and Abednego had worked and prayed toward the peace and prosperity of the place they were exiled, they were told to bow down to an idol image of their new emperor. Even though they risked all, and were thrown into a fiery furnace, they knew they couldn't render their worship unto Caesar. That was God's. They resisted. And their lives were saved. A king's eyes were opened, too. Who else could save in such a way, even from the power and the authority of the king?

And yet another: Daniel was a counselor to the emperor in exile. He didn't change the world because of which emperor ascended to the throne—he wasn't distracted by who was elected in which season. Instead, he served for peace and prosperity, and when he was persecuted for praying he kept right on praying, even trapped in a den of lions. Throughout his life, his devotion to God gave him favor and ability that far surpassed anyone else in the God-deprived society around him. God made Daniel stand out. Every king promoted Daniel in their court and government because they found him to be ten times more capable than any other person trained to serve in the kingdom.[4]

The Bible shows this, too: When Jesus teaches us to pray to the Father, it is "Your kingdom come, your will be done, on earth as it is in heaven."[5]

Finally, the later books in the Bible echo this: When Paul wanted to make clear what God did for us, he talked about a currency-like transfer, saying, "He has rescued us from the kingdom of darkness and transferred us into the Kingdom of his dear Son."[6]

YOUR TWO KINGDOMS

No matter where you are, you can choose which of these kingdoms to give your life to. Which one do you submit to, and which one do you try your best to influence? It matters which one comes first. If your heart is obsessed with the kingdom of Caesar, or the election of a president, or who is in charge of your province or state—and it is more important or urgent to you than the Kingdom of Jesus—then you've made a "carved image" of these rulers, too.

What if you made a list of the priorities, the obligations, the dreams, the values, and even the members of your family? Try to include everything that matters to you or takes up space in your day. Be honest. Be as complete as possible. Then ask God to help you make an accurate assessment. Which of these belong to God in your life, and which of these should belong to someone else?

Just as my wife has to move money from the savings account to cover the checking account, you could make some transfers, too. Some things could fit into both lists. Some things could fit into only one. But the longer list just might give you an honest account as to which kingdom comes first in your life.

14

SWITCHING SIDES

Am I too far gone to come back to God?
Does God write people off?

I want to pause here and answer the questions above, questions you may have. Perhaps you have doubts in your heart, and you wonder if something is wrong with you, like some glitch within you that makes you different or unfixable. You may think you are too far gone, that you have done something or continue to do something that means you are beyond God's reach.

Maybe where you come from, you don't see anyone else stepping up and breaking out. Abusers keep abusing. Drunks keep drinking. Addicts keep using. They teach their kids. The same cycles continue for generations. Maybe you have been a part of the same kinds of bad decisions for so long that you've just learned to cope and accept life the way it is.

Even if you tried to live differently, you know you'll face opposition and even hate from those in your life who don't want change. So instead you've jumped to the obvious conclusion: *God must be against me, too.*

I'm taking a moment to let you know that if you're still reading this, clearly God is trying to speak to your spirit. And he sees you leaning in, checking to see what he might have next for you. You're not too far gone. God's not done with you yet. He's right there with you.

Sound good? Now let's talk about a certain woman who had street sense. You might notice that the street she lived on feels a lot like yours.

A STREETWISE WOMAN

She may not have been well educated or rich, but she was connected, experienced, and streetwise. Most prostitutes are.

At some point, Rahab faced a decision too many women in history have faced, when they can't make ends meet and they come to the end of their rope. At that point they sell the only thing they have left of economic value: their bodies. This woman was accustomed to life in her hometown of Jericho. She might not have been high class, but she knew people from every class.

She knew the army and the police. She knew the government officials and the baker and the carpenter. She knew the priests of the temple perhaps best of all, because the selling of sex was not confined to the red-light district of her city. The name Jericho comes from the word for "moon." These people worshipped a pantheon of gods, the chief among them the moon god, and sexual acts with a prostitute were considered an act of worship. People would pay the temple and women like Rahab for these services. In the twisted religious and sexual economy of this time, it was considered a win-win-win: The payee gets to feel he is worshipping the deity while seeking pleasure, the temple gets their cut, and the sex slave gets to eat.

Rahab lived in a home built against the wall of Jericho. Like others without many resources, people found it made sense in that day to build a home with just three sides, as the wall formed the fourth.[1]

The whole city of Jericho had been watching over their walls at the coming hordes of the Hebrew people. They were well prepared. The spring had brought them ample rain to store up as drinking water, and they had taken in the harvest, so they were stocked up for a siege.[2] Jericho was ready for war, and they would do what many cities did in that day: wait out the enemy. If they could just survive behind their walls for months or even years, the enemy would need to leave eventually.[3] It was the primary strategy of the day and the very reason people like Rahab lived in the big cities of that region.

However, this enemy was a bit different. For a start, there was so many of them! Hundreds of thousands of Hebrews descended upon their region like locusts. But this strategy could be a problem for the Hebrews as well. The harvest was already taken in, so there would not be much to feed their horde.

There was much to fear, however, as the Hebrews already had a reputation for dispatching enemies with an almost cosmic force. Two major kingdoms had already fallen before them.

And now they were doing something very strange. Instead of building siege engines or digging beneath their walls, the Hebrews were marching around their walls as if they were in a holiday parade. God uses different tactics from the armies and kings of this world. The people of Jericho mocked them from their walls; the parade is supposed to come *after* the battle, not before.

But the opposing team had come to town, and everyone was sizing them up. I've been in that mode before, sizing up the opposition. It happened for me at a football game.

THE OTHER TEAM

Our Imperial high school football team had been great contenders, but not necessarily champions. For twenty years, I'd watched as they did well, but not well enough to win championships. But one year things started to click at a higher level— it had that special feeling you know only once you've been there. You can imagine that having a football team going to the playoffs is a pretty big deal in a town where the elementary school, middle school, and high school are all housed in the same building.

One of my pastor friends lives over in Atkinson, Nebraska, and I had gone to visit him that same year. Turned out that his son's football team was also having a very good year, so they got into the playoffs, too. We both wondered how far our teams would get. Turns out they got to face each other in the very first round of playoffs. One of our team's seasons was going to end abruptly, one way or another. You can imagine the ribbing and goading that went on between my friend and me. But I had the advantage. We were the home team; playing in our house was not going to be a walk in the park.

I sized up their team. They were impressive for sure, much

larger than our boys. It was late into our crisp northern plains autumn, and steam rose off the other team after their warm-ups. They stood on the sidelines and huffed out mist in the cold like caged bulls. They were a scary bunch.

Our guys were just a bit anxious about the first hits. But though our team didn't have the size they did, we had speed. It would be a contest between two philosophies.

After the kickoff, we got the ball and the team crouched there on the line, ready to hike the ball. From my spot in the bleachers I could see down the row of our linemen and theirs. At every position, the other team outsized us. They were bubbling with energy, on their toes, and ready to roll over us. But our players were on their toes, too. By that time in the season, our hometown Longhorns were getting accustomed to beating larger-sized opponents. And then came the shouts of our quarterback, who backed up off the line with the ball just as several of their huge defensive linemen started to push in.

Then came a handoff to our fullback, a shorter guy like me, who ran full tilt into the fray. Somehow our offensive linemen had pushed the momentum of the bigger men to the right places, and our fullback squeezed through the hole created. The large linebackers converged for a big tackle, but they were too slow, and then the fullback evaded the safeties, too. He ran and ran and ran, leaving them in the dust.

Touchdown!

Our side erupted in surprised joy. We scored in just one play up the middle. Our guys were good, but they weren't great, were they?

That day they were. Speed overcame size all night long.

When the night was nearly over, we put in our third-string players, and they still did well, but allowed the other team to get some points on the board. As the other team's huge men sulked off to the lockers, I looked up at the scoreboard's blaring lights against the dark Nebraska sky and saw the blowout score, ahead by more than fifty points. We had crushed them.

It doesn't matter how big you are, you can't tackle what you can't catch.

ON THE LOSING END

During halftime, I looked to the other stands, where the cheerleaders were sitting wrapped in coats and blankets, and the students had put away their big signs proclaiming their dominance, now just reminders of misplaced overconfidence. Parents huddled with each other, contemplating the night's loss at the end of their season, and the hard, long, silent drive home to the other end of the state.

They so badly wanted to be in our shoes, and I could sense what it would feel like to be in their shoes, in part because of my pastor friend sitting on the other side. That's a horrible feeling—to lose so badly.

You know one thing that never happens in these situations? Nobody ever crosses over to the other side, takes off their team's jersey, and switches sides to cheer for the opponent. No matter how bad it gets for your team, you don't switch teams. You can lose ten games straight and plan to bring a paper bag to put over your head in the eighth inning or the fourth quarter or third period because you just know that your guys are going to continue to stink, but what you don't do is bring the other team's jersey to switch to in case things go bad. That's a lack of loyalty. That's bandwagon-hopping. That's no true fan, is it?

Rahab did what so few others would ever even think to do: She switched teams. She dropped her Jericho jersey in the straw and walked over to the Hebrews. When a few Hebrew spies showed up to her door, she didn't report them to the authorities she knew so well; she sided with the opponent and helped them. Why?

For four reasons:

1. **She knew this was more than a game.** This wasn't a simple sports game. There was no ball or referee or scoreboard. This was an eternal matter. God was involved. "The Lord your God is God in heaven above and on the earth below," she told the spies.[4] She knew that the god of these Hebrews was *the* God of Heaven, who was for real on earth. She didn't betray the moon god of Jericho—there was no such god to betray in the first place. She was going from nothing to *something*, and no one to *Someone*.

2. **She knew the Jericho team didn't care about her.** The Jericho team had used her and abused her. She was trafficked for purposes that helped everyone around her while only giving her enough to eke by on, trapping her

until the day she would age out and become expendable. Examining her situation, she knew the other team would provide more hope for her than where she was. She realized that doing the same thing over and over and expecting different results is the definition of insanity, so she changed jerseys.

3. **She knew what God had already done for the other team.** Word of God's works had reached them—"the Lord dried up the water of the Red Sea for you when you came out of Egypt,"[5] she said, and then she listed off the many enemies that God had defeated for them. Because of this confession from Rahab, we find out the true hearts of the Jericho people: They are not confident while jeering down from behind their walls. In fact, they are terrified. "A great fear of you has fallen on us," Rahab reported, "so that all who live in this country are melting in fear because of you...When we heard of it, our hearts melted in fear and everyone's courage failed because of you..."[6]

4. **She knew the outcome of the game in advance.** Because of what God had done, and her faith that the Hebrew God was the true God, she told them of her faith: "I know that the Lord has given you this land."[7]

In this situation, the only wise thing to do is to leave the stands you're sitting in and switch teams. It isn't about loyalty to your home team; it isn't about being faithful to the other fans—it's about being *smart*. It's just about honesty. The team that opposes God and his people isn't worthy of your allegiance. It isn't even a real team anyway; it doesn't serve the true God. Their false gods and upside-down morality and self-consuming habits have used and abused you and others. They have expected and trained you to do the same. Have they really cherished you and added value to your life? It doesn't make sense to stick with them.

Rahab didn't do what so many of us are tempted to do. It is human nature to write people off and say, "You're dead to me." But she realized that God's nature might be different from that of the people she had lived with. Maybe it was worth the risk to see if God would give her a chance to live for him. Maybe she could be valued instead of used. After all, no one is so far gone that they cannot turn to God.

GOD SHOWS UP FOR REAL

So Rahab switched teams, and followed the instructions of the spies to put a scarlet cord in her window so that her home would be designated when the time came. It's good she switched teams. God showed up again like he had before, and the prophecy of the prostitute came true.

After the Hebrews marched around Jericho for the seventh time after seven straight days of marching once a day, they blew their trumpets and God moved in. The walls shook and came tumbling down. Archaeologists have found not only crumbled walls there, but also a section that did not fall. Many think this is because of a single scarlet cord hung from a window.

Rahab survived and joined the other team. When she crossed over, she switched teams confidently and engaged fully. She married a Hebrew and raised a family.

There's a story that follows the tale of Rahab in the Bible. A foreigner from another country settled in the lands of Israel. Her name was Ruth, from Moab. She worked in the fields, collecting leftovers to help her and her mother survive, as they were both widows. They were poor and, like most of the poor, they were unknown, unloved, and unnoticed.

But a man named Boaz noticed Ruth. He valued her, and made sure she had enough to eat. He even began to fall in love with her. After a legal process required by their culture, he became the "kinsman-redeemer" for her, a distant relative who could redeem the line of her family. They married and had children. Boaz was Rahab's son. No wonder Boaz could look on an outcast woman and see value—he was raised by the most important outcast prostitute in all of history.

That's a great story, but it doesn't end there. That prostitute, Rahab, became the great-grandmother of King David, and is listed in Matthew 1 in the lineage of Jesus Christ himself. In the New Testament of the Bible, Rahab is ranked as a hero of the faith alongside a few other important figures like Abraham and Moses.

God not only lets people come to him from all sorts of shady pasts and hardened lives, he forgives them and welcomes them. He even places them on his honor roll.

THE END . . . OF YOURSELF

How much of God do I need in my life?
Can't I just have a "little" religion in me?

I have become acquainted with a guy by the name of Perry Natarelli through a ministry in Buffalo, New York. When you see Natarelli and hear him talk, you are struck with what God has done in him, and you also get to see what a real mafioso-type guy looks and talks like. When I speak with him and see his neck, which seems thicker than his head, I'm just glad I didn't encounter him in a dark alley before Jesus encountered him.

From an early age, Natarelli got involved in drugs and organized crime. His father was already involved in this work and so Natarelli felt like he grew up in the "family business." He ended up dealing drugs in the 1980s, and found that because drugs were around, it was easy to keep doing them.

He should have died more times than he can count. But he says that God wouldn't let him die—kept giving him chances to respond to his grace. Natarelli had massive heart attacks.

His lung collapsed half a dozen times. This is the kind of stuff that happens to your body when you never miss a day of doing drugs in twenty-five years. He was so messed up physically at one point that he was on life support, and as his mother was sprawled out at his bedside, she prayed that God would take her instead of him.

On April 20, 1996, at eight fourteen in the evening, Natarelli came to Christ at the age of thirty-eight. He says of the experience, "I didn't go looking for Jesus, he came looking for me."[1] In that moment, God redeemed someone who had rebelled against him for decades, someone guilty of crimes against others who had destroyed his own body in the process.

God makes the impossible probable.

The book of Revelation speaks of the saints in Heaven, saying, "...they have defeated him by the blood of the Lamb and by their testimony. And they did not love their lives so much that they were afraid to die."[2] This Scripture speaks to me about lives like Natarelli's. His testimony is something that defeats the enemy. Sometimes people get to the end of themselves and turn to God, as Natarelli did. It's as if the extremity of their sin and the depth of their rebellion convert them—they have gone so low, they can't go any deeper. Like Saul in Acts, the conversion is so dramatic that even the church has trouble believing God has done it.

Charles Spurgeon put it this way: "I have a great need for Christ. I have a great Christ for my need." Jesus is so great he can take the great needs we have and turn them on their heads, making us strong in our weakness. As it says in 2 Corinthians, "My grace is all you need. My power works best in weakness."[3]

Some of us come to the end of ourselves. We hit rock bottom. We admire those who come back from this abyss and come to Christ—those who have learned to let go of themselves and trust God. But all of us can do this, and we don't have to hit rock bottom first. We can take up our cross. We can deny ourselves. It doesn't take addiction to come to the end of yourself. It doesn't take tragedy. It takes faith and trust in God. We move from negotiating with God to surrendering to him.

Selfishness must be overcome, and then God will say to you, "The end of you is not the end of me." When I was at the end of myself and worried for my son's life, I sensed God saying, "I'm God and you're not—and that is my child. You're just taking care of him for me."

BETTING ON GOD

I'm not a betting man, but I understand the simple idea of wagering. Imagine this: I flip a coin and ask you to call it, heads or tails. If you call heads and it comes up heads, then you win a brand-new car. If you call heads and it comes up tails, then you don't get the car, and you must pay me a hundred bucks. The upside to calling heads is huge here, obviously. Nobody is going to play a coin toss with you like this anytime soon.

If you call tails, and it comes up heads, then you keep your hundred bucks, but I take away your car. Of the four options in the bet, if you call tails and it comes up tails, then I give you a hundred bucks, and you've doubled your money to two hundred.

This is the logic behind Blaise Pascal's "wager" philosophy in faith. It's a way of thinking about faith in terms of the practical benefit. As Pascal said, "God is, or He is not."[4] There are only two sides of this particular coin. Pascal says the coin is already flipping, and time is short to choose your bet. "You must wager," he says. "It is not optional." Pascal makes the stakes even more stark than I did above: "If you gain, you gain all; if you lose, you lose nothing. Wager, then, without hesitation that He is...there is an eternity of life and happiness to be gained."

I think there are much better reasons to choose faith than just this. In reality, this wager is just a simplistic way to choose to believe some god exists (not necessarily the God of Heaven). Pascal was a brilliant mathematician who lived four hundred years ago, and his thinking was revolutionary for its time, but this is not why I have chosen God. However, I do think there are those who come to the end of themselves who have very little to lose, and they think through this wager on God. They can feel the coin flip inside them, and they choose God.

Have you reached the end of yourself? Are you close to hitting rock bottom? Or perhaps you've hit rock bottom before, or know someone who has. I think it makes perfect sense to bet your life on God, when you have no other options before you.

The reality is that those who hit rock bottom are given the gift of knowing what we all deny. We think we are self-reliant, we think we are doing fine...but we have all hit rock bottom in our sin, and in the long term we all depend on God for everything, whether we know it or not. In some sense, the wisest people in the room are those who have come to the end of themselves. They look down and out—but they are closer to God's truth than the rest of us. The first shall be last, and the last shall be first, Jesus told us.

GOD IS NOT YOUR COPILOT

When you reach rock bottom, you don't decide to have God join your team. You don't think of adding God to your life. You turn your life over to God in complete surrender. I think that's why conversions like Natarelli's are so dramatic. God fills up an empty vessel so much more than those of us who would just like 10 percent of God in our lives. They end up living more powerfully than the rest of us.

I don't care what the bumper sticker says, God is not your copilot...You don't give God *permission*; you give him *control*. That is the invitation he has given you. Carrie Underwood's song is more accurate to the actual conversion experience, because when you're out of control you say, "Jesus, take the wheel"—not "Jesus, would you grab the map and give me advice as my copilot?" We have so little power because we only give God permission in our lives up until the point when God offends us somehow. We want God in our lives, but don't allow him to take over our lives.

Part of this is because we've believed the lie that says, "If I let God do what he wants with my life, he will make me do something I hate." My friend Phil calls this the greatest lie in the world today that does the most damage. I have found repeatedly that while God may give you something that is difficult and stretching, the reality is that when you trust God, you find out you love following him, even in the stretching times. Nothing is more fulfilling than to surrender your life to God. Don't believe the big lie that God will just make your life dull, boring, and unfulfilling. In truth, God brings excitement, vision, and fulfillment.

HOW WHOLE?

One thing people wonder at times is why religious types talk about God in such extreme terms. It is easy to think someone like me is making a mountain out of a molehill. "Can't I have just a little of this in my life?" "Why does it seem like I must go whole hog into the Jesus stuff?" "Can't I just go to church occasionally, and be okay?"

I hear those questions, and I think they are legitimate. I agree sometimes Christians can sound a bit fanatical. Perhaps we're phrasing the question wrong. I'm not trying to convince you to be some extreme person. I just want to ask you one question: How whole do you want to be?

There is a great Hebrew word often used as a greeting, so you may have heard it before. The word is *shalom*. Most people talk about it meaning "peace," but another one of its meanings is "wholeness." Anyone who has heard the Christmas story knows of the angels saying the birth of Jesus would bring "peace on earth." We're prone to think that this means "no war." But for you, it means he brings shalom into your life. He brings *wholeness*. Whatever is broken in your spirit, he makes whole again. When life is shattered into a million pieces, he can put things together again and make meaning out of the mess.

Will life still be messy? Of course. But it begins to make sense and fit together, so your mind isn't shattered by it.

I ask you not to be extreme, I ask you what you want. How whole do you want to be? Fifty percent whole doesn't sound very whole to me. Jesus wants it all, because he wants to make all of you whole.

I WAS, NOW I

Jesus healed a man born blind in John 9. He was at rock bottom and had nothing to do but beg for his bread. God took this guy who'd been at the end of himself for decades—since he was born, in fact—and changed everything for him. It sparked a big debate with the religious leaders of the time, who brought the man before them like a courtroom witness. They asked him all about the man who healed him, trying to get the man to say Jesus was a sinner. He didn't quite know what to say, so he just said: "Whether he is a sinner or not, I don't know. One thing I do know. I was blind but now I see!"[5]

I love the simple testimony of this man, and I love how a testimony of a life changed like Perry Natarelli's proves the point of God's power. Instead of it being a lot of talk, it's a sign that God does indeed change lives. Maybe you're not a former drug-dealing organized-crime member, or you're not a person born blind and now you see, but perhaps God has changed you in some way already. Are you able to give a testimony to that?

It's fun to phrase it the same way the man born blind did in

John 9. He said, "I was blind, now I see." Can you fill in the
blanks the same way? "I was _____, now I _____."
If you asked groups of people this same question, they could
give a testimony to God's changing grace in a variety of ways.
Here are a few of their answers:

- I was a thief, now I give.
- I was physically broken, now I'm healed.
- I was wasting away, now I'm fulfilled.
- I was unforgiving, now I forgive.
- I was confused, now I have purpose.
- I was critical, now I'm understanding.
- I was arrogant, now I'm humbled.
- I was rejected and sad, now I'm accepted and joyful.
- I was insecure, now I have an identity.
- I was afraid, now I'm bold.
- I was lonely, now I'm loved.
- I was inadequate, now I have worth.
- I was running away, now I'm home.
- I was religious, now I'm saved.
- I was a worrier, now I trust in God.
- I was fearful, now I'm peaceful.
- I was addicted, now I'm free.
- I was broken and depressed, now I have joy.
- I was self-driven, now I'm Spirit-directed.
- I was ashamed, now I'm proud.
- I was tricked into sin, now I'm forgiven and free.
- I was passing the buck, now I take responsibility.
- I was in the dark, now I'm in the light.

- I was empty, now I'm being filled.
- I was bound, now I'm free. [6]

Do any of those describe your story? If so, circle it. If not, fill in these blanks for yourself:

I was _____, now I _____.

16

HAVING GOD'S BACK ON TRUTH

Does God really need me to speak to others about him?

M any years ago, when I was fresh out of college and only needed to shave once a month, I became a youth pastor. This job meant that all the teenagers in the church were my "congregation," and as almost every youth pastor finds out, the real key is connecting with kids at the high schools.

As I've mentioned, here in Imperial, the high, middle, and elementary schools are all in the same building. Back when I was a youth pastor, I was in a pretty sizable city with seven different schools to visit, so I worked hard to connect with kids in those schools, and jumped through all the hoops to be an official visitor at each one.

One thing I had to be intentional about was relating to the teenage girls in an appropriate way. I found the best thing to do was to come to the high school during their lunch hour, and go to the cafeteria as a visitor. The girls from my youth group would invite me to eat at their table, and then invite their friends to eat with us. It worked well because it was a safe and public place to meet. One time I visited Tina's school, and her lunchroom was quite the war zone of teenage drama.

I don't know how the lunchroom was when you were a kid, but I always found lunch to be a brutal time of separating the school into groups that would torment each other. Some make fun of how we try to protect kids these days, but I think most of us realize that things went way too far back in the day with bullying and taunting.

In Tina's cafeteria, there was a table of "cool kids" in one place, and then there was a table in the corner where all the outcast kids sat. It included those with disabilities, a few with learning challenges, and other types of kids you might guess would be there. The cool-kid lunch table would mock and yell at the other table—even while I was around. Even across the lunchroom as I entered I could hear what was happening, and it bothered me. I went over there to connect with one girl from my youth group, Debbie, who was at that outcast table.

Debbie was born with Down syndrome, and she struggled in school—but in our youth group she was a wonderful presence each week. She would stand right up front in the worship time, raise her hands, and sing her lungs out to Jesus. It was a beautiful thing to see, and it inspired our whole group to worship more meaningfully.

I sat down at Debbie's table next to her and began to chat with her friends. It was astonishing to me to hear the jeers and treatment of those at the table as the cool kids passed by, including the looks they gave these already challenged students. I was sitting right there among them, starting to realize what it might be like to be one of them, as I looked at their lunchroom world through their eyes for a moment. Other students started attacking me, swearing at me, and calling me names as well, since I was sitting with them. As an adult, you think you can handle these things, but the culture of that room was so hurtful that I even got dragged into it.

Tina went to the same school as Debbie, but Tina's life was quite a bit different. While Debbie's parents were strong Christians in my church, Tina's home life was much rockier. I knew Tina before she even came to my youth group because she lived on our street. She would notice I was cleaning up toilet paper strewn about in my trees from time to time (yes, that is one of the downsides of being a youth pastor—kids think it's hilarious to "TP" your trees occasionally). Once she found out I was a youth pastor, I invited her to come, and later she did, attending the youth group consistently for about a month. Each week, she would see Debbie there worshipping in front, and got to know her.

SCHOOL FIGHT

About two months after I had first seen the lunchroom division in Debbie's school, I visited again. This time I was running late, so the kids had been dismissed from the cafeteria. I went around the corner between two buildings the kids were walking from, and I came upon an ugly but familiar scene. It was a fight, just like you might imagine from your school days. All the kids were in a crowd and yelling out things at the fighters.

I stopped in my tracks, not quite knowing what to do. There were no teachers around. Should I stop the fight? Should I yell out something? What if they didn't listen to me? I wriggled my way through the crowd of kids and finally came up on the inner circle cleared out for the brawl. It was two teenage girls, already on the ground, tearing at each other's hair and punching each other.

I dove in and started to break them up. As I did, I realized that the girl who appeared to be winning the fight was familiar; beneath the sweaty hair was Tina from my street and youth group.

I got them separated then calmed down, and the crowd, now with nothing to watch, dispersed. As I tried to get out of Tina what was happening, I noticed another familiar face over on the steps near an entrance. It was Debbie, and she was crying, too. I finally discovered what was happening...the girl Tina was fighting had been picking on Debbie continually, pestering her. The girl wouldn't leave Debbie alone.

Tina said, "I told her if she didn't leave Debbie alone I was going to fight her." Apparently, Debbie even owed the girl some money, and Tina had gone so far as to pay back that debt herself, and the girl still wouldn't let up. So Tina fought her to defend Debbie.

I was in a tough spot. Youth pastors aren't supposed to encourage their kids to fight, but I was torn between getting Tina in trouble and just giving her a huge high five.

Was Tina behaving in the perfect way in defending Debbie? No, but I tell you what, for someone who was so young in her faith, she sure had a good sense of justice and defending the weak. She stood up for her new special-needs friend from youth group when she was targeted by a bully.

DEFENDING JESUS

Because of the movie about my family, I end up in some odd conversations from time to time with people I wouldn't meet back home. One time I was at a dinner with a woman who bluntly told me she disagreed with what we were doing. She specifically objected to the way my son would talk so confidently about his experiences, especially when they involved what a person had to do to be saved and go to Heaven. She preferred more spiritual wiggle room in these interpretations.

I explained that all my son was doing was sticking up for his friend, Jesus, as a little kid might imagine it. When others call into question the truth about Jesus, whom my son knows, then he's going to stick up for him—it's just the right thing to do. Wouldn't you want someone to do that for you? If someone says something untruthful about you behind your back, you would want a friend to stand up for you.

A lot of negative things have been said about our family, but even more hurtful are the times when people we thought were friends didn't stand up for us. God feels the same way. He wants us to stand up for his truth when others contradict it. Sometimes we just need to have guts like Tina and stand up for what's right. Even if we don't get in a hair-pulling fight over it, we can at least use our words to make sure God isn't blamed inappropriately, or that the truth of Jesus Christ isn't distorted.

DEFENDING THE TRUTH

How should we go about defending the truth? Well, it is our job to do so if we are believers. The Apostle Peter told us to "always be prepared to give an answer to everyone who asks you to give the reason for the hope that you have." If we don't work a bit to be prepared, then we aren't ready to have God's back on truth. Of course, it is easy to overdo this defense; it's our job to defend him, but not our job to attack those who attack God. That's why Peter continued, saying, "...do this with gentleness and respect."[1]

While it is the job of every Christian, it is an expected role for Christian leaders to be ready to defend the truth. The Apostle Paul described part of his job as "defending and confirming" the message of Jesus Christ.[2] He required leaders in the church to "hold firmly to the trustworthy message as it has been taught, so that he can encourage others by sound doctrine and refute those who oppose it."[3] While it is possible to do this respectfully, we must not back down from having God's back.

This isn't about having all the answers, or speaking eloquently. I've seen my own son Colton do this when he was just barely a teenager when our movie came out. We were booked to go on one of the most popular talk radio shows for just twelve to fifteen minutes. The famous host started talking to us adults, and noticed that Colton was there looking a little bored (which he was). So he asked Colton a question, and Colton answered straightforwardly. The host was so interested in how this kid just spoke his mind about his faith in Jesus that he spent a whole hour talking to Colton. The producers were rushing around in the background trying to cancel or reschedule other people after us.

Then we went on a major prime-time television news show. The host wore a sport coat and tie above the table and comfortable shorts below it. He was playing catch with a football to entertain everyone during the commercial breaks. The interview was very direct, with open-ended questions. At one point, he asked, "So, Colton, do you think everybody goes to Heaven?" It could have all gone wrong except for a kind but honest answer from the tween in the room.

Wow, how would you like to be asked that on national television when you were in junior high school? To be honest, I was a bit taken aback that the host gave that deep a question right to this kid—my kid! But Colton didn't even pause. He said, "Um, no. Not everybody does go to Heaven. The thing that I saw was that everybody there loved Jesus. God really does love you, but we're too attached to things on this earth, and they aren't allowed in Heaven. But once we love Jesus, and we follow him, it's easier to let those things go, and we can enter Heaven."

I've thought about these issues long and hard and I've heard a lot of people try to answer that question in hundreds of ways. To this day, I don't think I've heard a better response, and it came from a kid. You see: God isn't looking for you to sound smart to those who ask tough questions, or even to attack them; he's just looking for you to have his back on truth, with your simple trusting faith. Don't be rude; be respectful and kind. But stand in love on what you know.

LUNCHROOM SHIFT

About a month after the schoolyard fight I visited Debbie and Tina's school again for lunch. I noticed that something had changed in the lunchroom. The cool kids still sat at the same table, but the tough girls from Tina's table across the room had moved. They were now sitting with the special-needs and outcast kids in their corner. I noticed that nobody insulted them or gave that table weird looks anymore. There was a new sheriff in the lunchroom with her posse—it was Tina from youth group.

17

WITHHOLDING THE CURE

Can't I keep my faith a private matter?

The BBC called him "the most hated man in America" and he was appropriately born on April Fools' Day in 1983.[1] He grew up in Brooklyn, New York, showing himself to be intelligent and ambitious, becoming a multimillionaire before he was thirty years old. He became so hated that he began auctioning off rights to punch him in the face on Twitter to raise funds for the cancer-surviving son of his deceased friend.[2] Our villain's name is Martin Shkreli.

Shkreli is the infamous CEO of the company that jacked up prices on Daraprim, a drug on the World Health Organization's essential medicines list. Why? Daraprim counters toxoplasmosis, an infection that is particularly threatening to pregnant women, those with weakened immune systems, and the elderly. It causes seizures, blindness, birth defects in babies of infected mothers, and, in some cases, death.

Once he got the rights to Daraprim, Shkreli raised the price on the drug 5,000 percent, from $13.50 to $750. That price is for just one tablet—$750 per pill.[3] He could do this because there wasn't any competition for Daraprim, and while others could eventually make it as well, they would have to go through a long process of Food and Drug Administration approval.

This meant that many could not afford the drug anymore, and they had no other options. This made business sense for Shkreli, because even if only one out of twenty continued to buy the drug (only the richest clients, of course), he would triple his profits overnight. He was arrested on allegations of securities fraud in 2015, is out on five-million-dollar bail, and as of now is awaiting trial, passing his time wheeling and dealing, taunting the masses who hate him on social media, somehow enjoying the dark corners cast by the media limelight.

We rightly despise Shkreli for making what saves lives unattainable to most. However, we don't think often about what we withhold that saves lives for eternity.

HIDING THE CURE

The life-transforming message we have in Jesus Christ saves lives. While Daraprim is an important drug, it doesn't save someone for eternity. We hold Shkreli responsible for pricing Daraprim out of reach for most, but for how many have we put the message of Jesus out of reach? We withhold the cure of Jesus Christ, which makes all things new in this life and the next life: "The one sitting on the throne said, 'Look, I am making everything new!'"[4] Our perspective would drastically change if we considered that we withhold the cure from those who need it.

We withhold the cure when we come across as so holier-than-thou that those far from God think they would not be welcome to have a spiritual conversation with us.

We withhold the cure when we do not listen to the Holy Spirit prompting us to start a conversation about Jesus with someone—and we choose our own comfort zone over letting them hear about the love Jesus has for them and the good things he wants to do for their lives, their families, and their eternities.

We withhold the cure when our churches become places that do not welcome the marginalized and the down-and-out—when church becomes a place for those who have it all together.

We withhold the cure when we choose to confine the life-saving message of Jesus Christ to only those people who have already heard, neglecting the seven thousand unreached people groups around the world who have never heard, and the one million communities without one local church.[5]

We withhold the cure when we do not proclaim Jesus in a challenging situation, even with someone who is attacking us for our faith. Remember that the Bible has stories of those who persecuted the faithful at first. How many future great believers do we withhold the cure from by considering them a lost cause? Some start off as enemies and end up as our best allies. No one is a lost cause in Christ's cause to love the lost. All people matter to him. So, people need to matter to us.

Some defend their withholding by saying that their faith is

a deeply private thing they don't want to force on others. This is not a way to look at your faith and it certainly doesn't match the way Jesus talked about it. The message of Jesus that changes your life is deeply personal, but it can never be entirely private. This isn't like your personal opinions on politics or entertainment, like confessing who you voted for in the 1990s or which movie star is most attractive to you. In fact, complete atheists who truly understand the gravity of what you believe would think you didn't care about them if you did not share Jesus with them.

We do all kinds of things to celebrate our girlfriends and boyfriends when we're young. A girl will wear a guy's letter jacket or class ring. A guy will put a girl's picture in his locker, or get a tattoo of her name. We mark a relationship's progress by changing our social media status as "in a relationship" with someone. It always seems odd to me that we will publicly celebrate our prom date, but not celebrate our relationship with Jesus. If you've decided to make Jesus your Lord and Savior, then it makes sense to be publicly grateful.

A FLASH FROM THE PAST

I've been the fire chaplain in the state of Nebraska since 2002. Because of this, I end up traveling all over the state for various functions. Sometimes they are difficult, like a funeral for a fireman who died in the line of service. At other times, I get to do some pretty interesting stuff and travel to all kinds of venues. I've been at banquets where we've honored fire personnel for their sacrifices. Sometimes I get trained to do things I normally would never get to do because of the role. And best of all, I've set up speakers and a stage and talked about Jesus all over the place, since I have that platform as fire chaplain to communicate in these settings.

From time to time we have what's called fire school: Firefighters come from all over the state to a single location for training. Of course, it also is a chance for some of the best tailgating in the world. Where I come from, having a barbecue means the three B's...brats, burgers, and lots and lots of beer. Even though I don't drink personally, I enjoy the conversation and chance to build relationships in these settings.

At one fire school, the parking lot was packed with cars. I suppose it's more accurate to say it was packed with pickup trucks. The tailgates were open and everyone was hanging out enjoying themselves. And I was there connecting with people. The guys I was hanging out with know I'm not just a typical firefighter, but also the chaplain.

Pretty soon a female firefighter staggered up to us. She was clearly drunk. For some reason, she walked right in front of all of us and looked me dead in the eyes, and then raised up her shirt—bare for all to see.

As you might imagine, this was not the kind of greeting I was used to getting in my line of work. The whole group of us were stunned, but then all the other guys around me, knowing this was a bizarre experience for me as a pastor, busted up laughing.

I grew up being told, "If you can't say anything nice, don't say anything at all." So, I just stood there and said nothing. Speechless.

At this point the woman registered the fact that the guys were giving me a hard time, and so she looked at me and realized, "Oh no, you're the chaplain!"

She paused a moment and said, "Oh well."

As they laughed hysterically, one of the firemen said to the group, "It's the only time we remember Reverend Burpo shutting up and not saying anything." (I don't much like it, these guys calling me "Reverend.")

A full two years later, we were at another state meeting and it happened that there was a terrible local fire. The volunteer firefighters all left to respond. With old architecture and not one fire wall to impede the flames, the fire moved quickly from one business to another. An entire city block burned to the ground that night. Our fire convention came to a halt because of the tragedy. Other departments arrived from miles away offering to take shifts.

My kids—who were just six and nine years old at the time—were with me there to sing on stage. I couldn't help with the fire because I was watching them. So we headed to a local firehouse to hang out. My kids quickly began playing on a foosball table.

The building was mostly empty. As the kids were playing, a woman came into the game room and started walking toward me. I couldn't believe it; she was the same lady from two years before at the tailgating party who had lifted her shirt!

I thought, *Oh no, I hope this isn't a repeat.* In my mind, I was telling her, *You see my kids right over here; I hope you haven't had too much to drink.*

She sat down next to me and out of the blue said, "Reverend, can I talk to you?"

PASSING ON THE CURE

The woman then opened up about the difficulties of her life and what she was going through. She felt like her family was falling apart, and confessed to several struggles with relationships.

Now, in my head, I was thinking that this had come out of nowhere. I was worried about what was happening. I mean, it's not often that the first time you meet someone, you see them topless, and then the second time you talk to them about spiritual things. But that's the way this one turned out. I reflected on the fact that I could have said so many things two years earlier to her, either to humiliate her, or to help me feel better about how humiliated I felt standing there with all the guys making fun of me. I am so glad I didn't do anything that would have pushed her away from the message of Jesus, nothing that might have withheld the cure from her.

I got to speak to her for a long time about how God could make a difference in her choices and relationships. I prayed with her, and we spent almost an hour together there in the firehouse with my kids playing nearby. She prayed that God would take over her life and she'd get into a fellowship with other believers so she might grow spiritually. She was on her way toward the cure.

WALK THIS WAY

When you live for God and you walk with God, you have so many opportunities to talk about God without being offensive. If you're positive and lift people up and aren't trying to gain attention for yourself, you begin to gather people around you. They notice that your attitude is different, and you get the chance to share Jesus with them.

It starts so simply: offering help, serving people, and beginning to pray for them. Then they start to share their concerns. If you ask if you can pray for them, they want you to, even if they don't believe yet. They respect that you do. They can see that you have hope and they don't. Yes, they see your faith, but often you need to break the ice, then begin to share why it is that you are different. You're not better than them, you just have Jesus in your life. As I said earlier, you're *better off*, but not *better than*, because of no virtue of your own—merely by the grace of God you've received.

I should point out that one thing you may encounter as you speak to those far from God is that some people hate positive folks—life irritates them, so avoiding those who have hope is sometimes the approach of the hopeless. If you surround yourself only with other hopeless people, it doesn't make you question your approach to life. You just think everyone is like you. But a hope-filled person changes the dynamic, and sometimes this is hard for the hopeless to endure. Their own vulnerability is compromised when you suspend their disbelief that hope is possible.

SHARE YOUR EXPERTISE

Whatever the case, be ready to offer the cure to those in need. While Martin Shkreli is one of the most hated men in America, the reality is that withholding the cure—the message of Jesus—is a far more villainous thing to do, with eternal consequences.

Everyone is an expert about at least one thing: themselves. No one knows all the answers to everyone's questions—or all of the Scriptures, for that matter. But everyone has expertise about their own experience. You know all about you. If you know that God has made a change in your life, you have something to share with others.

You can also start the conversation about things the two of you have in common. Jesus used fishing as a discussion starter with Peter all the time. Then when it was right, he asked Peter to put his boat into deeper water. I believe his Spirit will let yours know when the time is right to head out to deeper water, too.

18

MADE IN PRACTICE

What about all the difficulty and pain in my life?
What does God do about that?

Practice doesn't make you perfect, but it might make you better than the opponent you're facing in next Saturday's tournament. As a wrestler when I was young I tried to apply this, and in the years I served as a wrestling coach I constantly communicated it to my athletes. It's something I still get to do with my son Colton, who is a wrestler today. As a wrestler, you win the match in practice, not in the match itself. The match is just where you execute what you've trained your body to do. Champions are made when the stands are empty.

A wrestler will focus on diet, running, and lifting, and that's all before the practices even begin—that's the off-season stuff. If a wrestler is going to be a true competitor, it will be more about what he does to prepare than how he performs in the match. The wrestler who tries to beat himself in practice every day is always the one most prepared before the championship matches even begin. A well-prepared wrestler was already winning back when nobody was watching. Your spiritual life works the same way.

AIMING FOR VICTORY

First, let's clarify what we're aiming for. In sports, you don't practice hard unless you know why you're doing so. You must have a goal. If athletes are trying to make it to the Olympics, then they train like people heading to the Olympics. If they are trying to lose twenty-five pounds, then they train like folks trying to lose weight.

What are you aiming at spiritually? It's important to know this. As has been said, if you aim at nothing, you'll hit it every time. Are you aiming at *nothing* spiritually? Are you just hoping to "break even" in this life, assuming it will all sort out in the end?

I'm here to tell you there's more to life than that. There's more to life than just aiming at Heaven as well. Know this— you can have victory. You can beat the Enemy. He's not so impressive. He doesn't have Jesus in his corner. You do.

I've heard a story about the evangelist Smith Wigglesworth who is said to have woken one night in his bed and turned to the corner to see the grim and fearful sight of Satan himself in the room, ready to do his worst. Wigglesworth took one look at who it was and said aloud, "Oh, it's only you!" Then he turned over toward the wall and went back to sleep.

Don't you just love that kind of spiritual attitude? If only we all understood that Satan has no power over us that we don't let him have. The name of Jesus is more powerful than anything that might be thrown at us.

Part of practice is clarifying that you want to win, that you wish to beat the Enemy and have victory. If you know this in your soul: You don't just want to *survive* life; you want to *thrive* and want the power of a real God to support you and give you victory. Then you will be ready for the next part. Easy wins might come. But hard wins are earned in practice. Remember: No one scores a victory in practice, but no championship comes without it.

CHARACTER MUSCLES

When speaking of the hardships we face in life, the Bible says, "...we know that in all things God works for the good of those who love him, who have been called according to his purpose."[1] It doesn't say *some things* are worked out for good, or that *only the good things* work for the good. No, it says "all things."

Somehow God is using the junk of life to make you better. How?

Think of your character as muscles you are building in your experiences. You already know this to be true of your past experiences, don't you? You are better at certain things in life now because of what you've gone through in your past. What you went through *back then* is what makes you better *right now*. So, why wouldn't that be part of what God is doing in you right now in the experiences and challenges you are facing?

Those who begin to truly grow their character intentionally develop the ability to see this by looking to the past, and they also begin to sense it in the present. And the most spiritually practiced among us develop such deep character that we even look at the future this way, so we become downright fearless.

When my son Colton was just a freshman, he was messing around during music class on a break and climbed up a tree. The limb snapped, and he fell and broke his arm. The teacher was furious, in part no doubt because music class doesn't often have such severe injuries.

The cast was removed the week after scheduled practices began. It came as no surprise to anyone that his arm was tender and weak. Most wrestlers would admit that the freshman year is already brutal enough with two good arms. Colton's left arm looked about half as thick as his right one. Then the following year, he cut his left pointer finger at the beginning of the season. The ER misdiagnosed the depth of the cut. They stitched him up. Told him to wait two weeks then go back to wrestling. Well, his finger never worked again. It turned out that his tendons were severed. They died within his hand and Colton wrestled his sophomore year with only one good arm again.

Before his junior year, Colton had to have two surgeries to rebuild his hand. After one surgery, I remember holding him down as the nurse pulled forty-seven stitches from his palm and pointer finger. If we ever have to do that again, I'm bringing someone else to help me pin him to the table. But again, he got released from therapy right before the season started.

Going into his senior year, Colton had a problem because his left arm had never been as tested and strong as the right. It was his weak spot. And this was his only chance to wrestle in high school with two strong arms instead of one.

I warned him, "Son, you cannot rebuild three years of atrophy in three weeks before the season starts." Focusing on dumbbell lifts, he worked very hard and very long in the off-season to bring both arms up to speed and strength. Overtraining had to make up for years of underusing.

I sure wanted him to have a good year. After years of asking his dad to let him quit, he was now working hard to get out in front. Fully healthy, and with two strong arms, he started succeeding and winning matches. This year his enemy wasn't injury; it was preparation. It might have been a struggling summer of testing rather than time off for swimming, but it made him who he is, and I think he worked harder than many others because of it. He ended up winning three matches for every one he lost this year, finishing just one place short of qualifying for the state tournament at districts.

This is what God wants to do with you. I stress this point to athletes: You must face weight resistance to build muscle. Nobody ever got stronger without resistance. Atrophied spiritual muscles need to face resistance to grow character. Those who have faced more resistance in life often have deeper character. Those who have experienced more pain have a higher pain tolerance. They've just worked out those character muscles.

It is hard to find a person in the Bible who didn't have a major character-testing season as a part of their story, where God forced them to grow some character muscles. Noah faced the mockery of his community, which prepared him for the solitary journey of building the Ark and then starting a new community after the flood. Jacob struggled under the shadow of his brother and connived his way through life, only to be broken by God for a purpose. Joseph was sold into slavery by his own brothers, then betrayed by his master's wife in Egypt, only to be forgotten by those he helped in prison. All this prepared him to be a savior during drought not just for his family, but also for the entire region.

These are just a few notable examples in only one book of the Bible, Genesis. If I went deeper into that book, or further through the other sixty-five books of the Bible, we'd see examples everywhere we turn of God using the people's experiences, often very dismal and dark, to prepare them for the future.

We mirror this in our television, movies, and books. No hero is a victor at the beginning. We instinctively want to see them go through hardship first. The novelist Kurt Vonnegut told us of this secret in writing when he said, "No matter how sweet and innocent your leading characters, make awful things happen to them, in order that the reader may see what they are made of."[2] This works on us because we internally already know that hardship is just the preface to victory. That journey is not just "a story"; it is *the* story of life that God wired us for. We know that practice matters, and we're building character there.

SITTING THE BENCH

One of the best-known characters in Scripture is King David. But the interesting thing about David is that he is anointed in 1 Samuel 16, and then you keep reading and discover that he doesn't become king anywhere in the rest of that entire book. You have to keep reading into the second book of Samuel to find him becoming king.

The guy waited twenty years for that to come true—and he didn't force it to happen; he waited for God to make it happen. He somehow knew that he wasn't ready, and God would grant him the victory when he was. By the time David was truly prepared for victory and power, he wielded it with humility. He had to sit the bench for a long time before God determined he was ready. That's what God often does with us. Those seasons build character muscle.

MY PRACTICE ROOMS

Let me tell you how this has all worked in my life. The reality is that God had me serving in the middle of nowhere for decades without getting any attention or credit for it. I feel like I was at the breaking point many times, financially, physically, spiritually, and emotionally. I think those were times when God was building character in me to withstand what would happen so publicly with *Heaven Is for Real.*

When you think about it, perhaps I was just the right person to have that happen to. One of the struggles of having a movie made about your family is that you are suddenly in the public eye. But all pastors—especially those in small towns—will tell you that their families are already always living in a glass house. So it wasn't the fact that we were under scrutiny, it was the scope of the scrutiny that changed. All the struggles I went through were just building the character to handle that attention without losing our focus on Christ (or losing our minds in the process). Many don't survive that shift. But God helped us through it. I didn't know what was coming, but God did. He knew the character muscles we needed to grow in advance.

I think some of the hardest things we faced were just like practice. I've noticed that true champions will push themselves to the very limit in practice, and then go even further. Why? Are they just sick in the head and like it? No. It's because they know a point will come in the match when they are pushed beyond their limit, and they want to know what that feels like in advance. They want to be familiar with what they can do when they have an empty tank.

There is an allure to fame, a sense of grandiosity that is easy to succumb to. I think God shielded me from much of this after years of people shaming me and making me feel like I wasn't worth anything. It started in my home with my father, and then it continued as I became a bi-vocational pastor.

Some would tell me right to my face, "You're wasting yourself by being a bi-vocational pastor. That's for people who can't do anything else." Maybe people thought they were protecting me, but saying that to anyone is just horrible. We shouldn't devalue people like that. God knew that I needed to pursue a path that wasn't in the limelight, that wasn't "successful" in many eyes, so that when I experienced success it wouldn't go to my head, and I would distrust that success and the way people treated me differently for no good reason.

The money is part of all this. When I first came to Imperial nineteen years ago, I was given just $169 a week. Because of this I told the church leaders I would have to work on the side. We moved into a house that needed a lot of work. I trapped seven mice in one day in that house not long after we moved in.

People in the church said to me, "Why do you love money so much that you can't just live on what we give you?" Um, really? We were on the verge of bankruptcy more than once, and the health bills for Colton came on top of all that. In many ways, it got worse right before it got better for us, which is part of the story of *Heaven Is for Real*, the story of our lives.

And get this: It is the story of *your life*, too. God is using this stuff, whatever it is, in *your* life, to prepare *you* for what's next. He's not just making you go through it to see what you're made of; he's letting you go through this so *you* can know what you are made of and what you can do in the future. He's not just going to get you through; he's going to work through you like never before. That's what happened for me. God prepared my character in the practice room of life. He'll prepare you, too.

YOU NEVER KNOW

In the end, you just never know what God is up to, and how he brings back what happened earlier in your life to use you in the future. I have a colleague and friend named Randall Wallace whom I have grown to respect greatly. He wrote the screenplays to *Braveheart* and *Hacksaw Ridge*, wrote and directed *We Were Soldiers*, and directed the movie *Secretariat*. He has some amazing work to his credit. The interesting thing I learned about my friend Randall is that early in his life he went to seminary, feeling called to study for the ministry. That wasn't the path he took in his life eventually, but he always wondered what place that had in his future.

We worked together on the movie *Heaven Is for Real*, which

he wrote and directed with such a gifted touch, and with great honor to the source material, my book, and the source behind the experience, God. I was so impressed with his ability to do something so many doubted was possible in Hollywood: treat my story with respect but also make a great movie out of it.

At one point Randall and I went to visit his mother's grave site together. He told me all about his family growing up, and his seminary days. He told me of pain he faced and how God seemed to be preparing him all these years. Even though he had written *Braveheart*, one of the most iconic movies of all time, he still wanted something else. He turned to me and said, "Todd, I think I waited my whole life to write this movie, *Heaven Is for Real*. I left seminary to do this kind of work: to use film to change people's lives. Now I get to do it."

19

FRAMED GOD

If God's so big—why doesn't he crush evil right now?
Why doesn't he intervene?

When I speak to a crowd, I often ask them if they think Jesus was right when he said, "In this world you will have trouble."[1] Yep, everyone I've ever asked thinks Jesus was right about that one. We have some big-time trouble in this world.

But there was another time Jesus talked about trouble... more specifically, the end of trouble. Jesus was seen in a vision on a throne, descending to earth, and he said, "Look, God's home is now among his people! He will live with them, and they will be his people. God himself will be with them. He will wipe every tear from their eyes, and there will be no more death or sorrow or crying or pain. All these things are gone forever." He continues with this amazing line: "Look, I am making everything new!"[2]

That sounds great to me. This world comes with a whole lot of trouble, we all agree. But a day is coming when there will be no more tears, and all things will be made new.

Wherever I go I find that what cuts to our core the deepest, what makes us long for that day when tears will be wiped away, has to do with those we love the most. Our great struggles are within our own families. We cry out for children in pain, or who are wandering away. We pray for parents who are sick or dying, or spouses who are hurting or hurting us.

We struggle with how those closest to us are in pain, or how they cause us pain. They let us down, or we let them down. This is where the rubber meets the road. I want to talk about a situation just like that.

NO ANSWER

In my town, there was a young woman whose family was struggling. I'll call her Danielle. She prayed and fasted for many weeks, asking God to do something in her family. Right after these weeks of prayer, Danielle's father-in-law got into serious trouble, and a warrant was issued for his arrest. As they served the warrant, a gun battle ensued, and he was shot dead by the police. On top of this pain, he shot a police officer who was delivering the warrant. The officer was in critical care for weeks, barely surviving.

This was after many of us had prayed hard for Danielle's family. Danielle, with no surprise, was the one woman who had prayed and fasted with the greatest determination. She reminded herself of how her painfully desperate prayers had worked before. Trials come to all of us. They are plural. I don't know of anyone who would say that they have had just one trial in their life. Danielle couldn't say that, either.

After losing one child to miscarriage at thirty weeks, the following pregnancy ended at only week twelve. Danielle was at a spot where she was going backward instead of forward. During her next pregnancy, she prayed more fervently and powerfully than she had ever committed to pray before. Her prayers worked. Her beautiful son was carried to full term.

But what happened with the prayers offered for her father-in-law? She couldn't fast when she was pregnant for fear of endangering the child, but she could and did take that step this time. Adding fasting to her arsenal of fervent prayer, she had the faith to believe God would again give her the answer she was praying for. She hadn't been praying for a shoot-out. What went wrong?

What are we supposed to do when this happens? When we do things right, we honor God, and things like this still happen. It makes me ask, "Was it better for me not even to try so hard?" God's lack of an answer sometimes feels like a slap in the face.

The Bible says, "The one who is in you is greater than the one who is in the world."[3] It means that God is greater than the Enemy. But at times like Danielle's crushingly bad answer to her prayers, I start to ask God why he doesn't prove that truth a little more often. Why isn't his Enemy and mine being overpowered?

Then God reminds me about a subtle but powerful difference in some of my "asks." Just as for Danielle, it is a difference that might explain one of our greatest frustrations in prayer. Are we asking God to move, or are we asking God to make somebody else move?

Jesus was asked to make Mary move by her sister Martha. Now, before you get confused, Mary was a common name back in the first century. This was not Mary the mother of Jesus. But both Mary and Martha were sisters and close friends of Jesus. They had what most people want from famous people today—access! Jesus was so involved in their lives, and their lives were so involved with Jesus, that Jesus invited groups of people to join him at Mary and Martha's home for dinner and a spiritual lesson.

But dinner became the problem; all the preparations without fridges and microwaves could be daunting, especially when a house is filled suddenly with unexpected guests. Both sisters were needed to pull off dinner, but one chose to sit with the guests in the front room and listen to Jesus instead of heading to the kitchen to cook with her sister.

Martha, the sister, got mad—mad enough to confront Jesus about it. You can feel the emotion in her words as she asked if Jesus even cared about her slaving alone. You would have probably said the same thing: "Make her come into the kitchen and help me prepare this meal!" If it was your sibling, you might have even been louder than Martha was that day.

Jesus refused. He said that Mary had made her own choice, and he wasn't going to force her to change it. Of course, we like the part where Jesus said that Mary had made the "better" choice. That part is understandable. We applaud Jesus for refusing Martha. But what if Mary or our sister or brother or parent or father-in-law was making a terrible choice; wouldn't Jesus have made them do the right thing? Why allow that choice? Doesn't he care?

Let me make this clear: This is just one answer to unanswered prayers. I would never say this distinction is the only reason why prayers and fasting don't turn situations in the direction we want them to turn. I've seen prayers and fasting do many powerful things. God's favor is a powerful difference-maker.

What I do want to say is that we have probably all been in this spot. We've all prayed for God to make that child, or that spouse, or that boss, or that bully at school stop and make the right choice. We think something like this: *If it's obvious that I'm right and Scriptures agree with what I am praying for, why don't my prayers get answered?*

In the middle of unanswered prayers, I can keep praying for God to influence people. God's influence is a powerful thing to pray for. The old-timers in church call it *conviction*. Believe me, God's conviction in response to a grandmother's prayer, a mom's prayer, a husband's prayer, a wife's prayer, or a child's prayer is powerful. Of course, the person you are praying for still gets to make their own choice, regardless of the weight of the guilt, the truth, or the circumstances that God lays upon them in response to our passionate and constant prayer.

DAD RULES

God gave people the freedom to choose, and so many of these tragedies come as the price of free will. If I were God, I likely wouldn't have chosen to give humans free will. It sounds a little more neat and tidy for me to have the power to have everyone do what I want them to do. (You might be thinking: *Well, it's a good thing Todd isn't God.* You would be right!)

But like the two criminals on the crosses next to Jesus, God gave each individual the right to make his or her own choice. He still gives each individual that right today, which means a lot of consequences come from our bad choices. Our families are hurt by our choices. Those we pray for don't respond to grace, and instead make the wrong call, and it breaks our hearts. I've thought about this a lot when it comes to my own children making their own choices.

In our home, our kids know that my wife has dozens of rules—she oversees things—but the kids also know that I have just three rules.

Rule 1: *I shouldn't have to tell you more than once.* When I tell the kids something, they know I'm just going to tell them once, and if there is a pause, I start counting…1, 2…Then they get running. They never like the consequences that happen after 3.

Rule 2: *Don't sass your mother.* This enforces all the rest of her rules, in a way. They know that if they make her mad, they make me mad. So, this is an important rule. It backs her up.

Rule 3: *If you and a sibling get physical, both of you are in trouble.* They know I don't care how it got started. They must solve their problems some other way than physically lashing out, hitting, or kicking, or they will both get in trouble.

My first two rules have always worked well, but this third rule just wasn't clicking. I was grounding them, punishing them, correcting them, but it wasn't working. So, a potato farmer I work with has some pretty tough-guy sons: One was a state-champion wrestler, and the other was a linebacker for the Nebraska Cornhuskers. I asked him how he kept those two brothers from tearing each other and this man's house apart. His first response surprised me and irritated me. He told me that the solution was easy. What? How could that ever be! Then he continued, "I make them hold hands in public as punishment." I thought: *Really?* That seemed odd to me at first. But over time as I tried it out, I found that public sibling awkwardness was the most effective punishment for my kids. It worked fast! My friend was a genius!

But years later the fighting shifted. Colton and Colby were locking horns instead of Cassie and Colton. After a bunch of yelling back and forth one day, I heard Colby and Colton arguing in the basement. Their noise obviously drowned out the noise I make when I come home. Unaware of my arrival, one of them interrupted the argument to say, "When Dad gets home we'll both be in trouble; we better figure this out now." I couldn't believe it. They were screaming at each other, but the prospect of holding a sibling's hand in public was still working. Once I figured out how to enforce the rule, they figured out how to live with it. Their choice was clear to me. The consequences were clear to all of us. Their choice was clear to them as well. But they still had to make the right choice for themselves.

I do all this to ground my parenting in something concrete in their life. They need something that doesn't shift. Straight lines teach character. Curvy lines teach deception and entitlement. Some parents teach their kids to expect to find loopholes or third or fourth chances instead of expecting responsibility from themselves.

I want my kids to make the right choices about things that will affect their lives in the future. They can still choose to make their own wayward choices, but I do my work to help them know what to choose. I think God works with us in the same way. Just as my kids can choose the wrong thing, people like Danielle's father-in-law can choose the wrong thing and cause very bad things to happen. God leaves the choice up to them.

Instead of dancing circles around God, trying to figuring out why bad things happen to good people, let's just admit that circumstances can be horrible in this life, and things don't always seem fair. God isn't out to get you; but he has promised to make all things new for you one day. Sometimes, nobody is being punished for a bad choice when bad things occur. Sometimes, life and the evil in this world we have already talked about strike innocent, undeserving victims. But sometimes, we aren't the victims. We chose our actions, and we received our consequences.

I don't make decisions; I just make choices. God has already decided the outcomes; I just choose whether to align with God or not. I choose whether to listen to and follow God. But I can't decide what God is going to bless and curse.

The decisions that decide my circumstances are out of my hands. God determines final outcomes. But I can still make choices to align with God or not, regardless of how it feels along the way.

BLIND UMPIRES

Let's talk about the book of Job for a minute. It has a fascinating story unlike anything else in the Bible. I'm guessing you haven't heard much about it before.

Job is a unique part of the Bible. It's not the kind of stuff you hear about on television. First off, the book of Job is *very* old. Because of a variety of qualities of this book, most think it is one of the oldest or perhaps even the oldest book of the entire Bible. The story is from before recorded history. When talking of when these events happened, you should think of things like the *Epic of Gilgamesh*, *The Ramayana*, the Egyptian *Book of the Dead*, or the *Code of Hammurabi*. I know, I know, these are old stale things that make you think of something Indiana Jones dug out of the Temple of Doom or something, but you get my point. This thing is super-old. It makes the Greek epics *Iliad* and the *Odyssey* seem like current events.

The first thing I want to point out about the book of Job is the idea of bad judges. Job 9:24 talks of how God blindfolds the judges of a land that falls into the hands of wicked leadership. It's as though all the people who are supposed to see what's wrong in the society lose sight of true justice.

I love the way Job 9:33 speaks of this next: "There is no umpire between us, who may lay his hand upon us both."[4] Have you ever been in a game where the umpire or referee was just ruining things with bad calls? Nothing wrecks a game like a bad umpire, and nothing creates a fair game quite like a good one. We need a judge who isn't blind, so we can play the game as intended. He leaves our part to us, and God calls 'em as he sees 'em.

Here's how the story goes down. First, Job is a great guy, the best guy. He's blessed and loves God. Others come to him for wisdom. But then God allows the Enemy to attack Job, and he loses his wealth, family, and even his own health. It's the worst bad-luck story in the Bible, except it isn't bad luck, it's an attack from the Enemy.

Then the story picks up some interesting dialogue from Job's friends. They range all over the place and they get more than a little wordy, but there's one part I want you to notice. Job has a friend named Eliphaz. He is an eloquent guy and analyzes Job's situation, as his friends are doing, and gives advice.

Eliphaz says this: "Can a mortal be innocent before God? Can anyone be pure before the Creator? If God does not trust his own angels and has charged his messengers with foolishness, how much less will he trust people made of clay!" Eliphaz is making the point that God is going to punish all, because he doesn't trust humans, and they are beneath his interest.

"They are made of dust, crushed as easily as a moth," Eliphaz continues. "They are alive in the morning but dead by evening, gone forever without a trace. Their tent-cords are pulled and the tent collapses, and they die in ignorance."[5]

This is some heavy stuff. And if true, it is sobering. I mean, this is Scripture, so it's true, isn't it? Eliphaz is giving sound wisdom, right?

Hold up. Look closer with me.

Earlier in this chapter, we find out that these words aren't even from Eliphaz, but he is reporting them as his advice. We read that Eliphaz says a "truth was given to me in secret, as though whispered in my ear."[6] So these words aren't his own.

He paints a picture of this "disturbing vision" that comes "at night, when people are in a deep sleep." Eliphaz is deeply troubled by this vision: "Fear gripped me, and my bones trembled." He sees something: "A spirit swept past my face, and my hair stood on end." He can't quite make out the shape of the spirit, but it was a form before his eyes, and in the terrifying silence of that moment it speaks, saying, "Can a mortal be innocent before God? Can anyone be pure before the Creator? If God does not trust his own angels..."[7] It continues just as above.

So, this "advice" from the friend of Job is from this "spirit." Who is this? I believe it was a spirit, just as Eliphaz says. In fact, it is an angel. He even speaks of how the angels aren't trusted by God—"If God does not trust his own angels." Who does this sound like? At minimum, this is a fallen angel, a demon of hell. It may even be a report from the Enemy himself, the same Enemy that used the form of a serpent to talk to Eve.

Isn't this just like the Devil? He would love to describe God to you in ways that erode trust. He wants Job, and you, to think that God doesn't care for you, that the relationship might be divided. He wants you to think pragmatically, to curse the situation you're in, and to throw your hands up in despair. This is what the Enemy wants. Don't listen to advice from those who might be getting their so-called wisdom from such sources. Job didn't listen to Eliphaz. Don't listen to the descendants of Eliphaz in your life, either.

Instead, listen to those who have seen God show up: the ones who know God is for real. Listen to those who didn't have to invent qualities God might have, but have experienced the real-deal Jesus showing up to make a difference in their lives.

When God shows up, you don't need to do mental gymnastics—you need an experience with God. You don't need to make up what God is like, you just need to put yourself repeatedly in a place where God can show up—and then respond. Pursue God, expecting him to show up.

Understand that while I'm known as the guy that talked about Heaven because his son experienced it, I am most passionate about God, not Heaven. If there were no God, there would be no Heaven. I'm worried that people want to go to Heaven, but they don't want to be with God; Heaven, however is just that: being *with* God. Hell is just the opposite: being *apart* from God.

If you're thinking that you've tried to pray, you've wanted a miracle and you didn't get it, then I want to address that, too. If that's how you feel, then put yourself in the shoes of Job. He had it bad, too. God didn't answer his prayers for a long time as well. He lost everything, and then some. Understand that it is not a binary problem. It's not just about you and God. There is a third person in the problem: the Enemy. Sometimes you're under attack. Sometimes the one who comes to rob, kill, and destroy does just what he intends to do: He robs you of joy, kills off your love, and destroys what you've worked so hard to preserve.

Don't blame God for what the Enemy has done. All I'm asking is that you don't give up on God, that you give him another chance.[8] I'm also asking you to open your eyes and see that God's enemy is your enemy, too.

FRAMING GOD

You might think it's only the church people who forget sermons, but we pastors do as well. I don't even remember what I was saying on the night a girl in my youth group spoke up. She was just thirteen years old at the time.

We were in the youth room of the church with about twenty students. Each week in our church bulletin, we have an application question that gets people thinking about the subject. We want people to engage with the sermon and apply it to their lives. Sometimes the teens respond with much better ideas than we adults do.

One young teen in our church turned in her sheet of paper where she had written her idea: "Satan hurts you, and then he frames God for it." We talked about it more deeply in the youth group time, because that was one of the most profound things I've ever read. The Enemy sets up a frame job on God, and we fall for it.

You see, this isn't just about you and God. There is an Enemy at play in the field of life. You don't have to choose just between blaming yourself or God. You can blame the Devil, and that's where most of the blame belongs. The Bible says it this way: "So don't be misled, my dear brothers and sisters. Whatever is good and perfect comes down to us from God our Father."[9] God gives good and perfect gifts. He's not the one causing horrible events in life.

There is one who only gives evil things, who only puts people on a collision course with chaos. That Enemy has power on earth to do this. Don't be confused as to who is the cause of evil. If the Enemy can convince you that the bad things in life are coming from God, then that is the greatest deception of all. He wants you to blame God.

The reality is that sometimes very bad things happen to good people, and good things happen to some very bad people. "For he gives his sunlight to both the evil and the good, and he sends rain on the just and the unjust alike."[10]

It's okay to wonder what God is up to. Go ahead and question God. I do. That's how we find answers from God. But in the end, know that even though battles may be lost, the war isn't over. Then hit your knees, praying with me for the true answers to come from God.

20

GOD IN ALL PEOPLE?

I should just look for the best in people, right?

She was a skilled and experienced publicist, getting me to open up about our story, as she no doubt had done with hundreds of people in the course of her work. She was the kind of woman that I felt I could talk to for hours.

Of course, as you know by now, asking me any questions about my story is likely to lead to a spiritual conversation. As our back-and-forth developed, I learned she was a bit of a religious dabbler, having sampled a bit of this religion and that from kabbalah to Buddhism. She respected them all, she said, but she wasn't committed to any one faith. In being evasive about spiritual things, she said in passing, "I believe God is in all people," in the hope of moving on.

Because it seemed like we were becoming friends, I stopped her at that point and said, "I just think there's no way you actually believe that."

Now she was stunned a bit, put off at my objection, since

this is what she claimed to believe. Expressing her philosophical viewpoint, she talked of how each person has good in them and she sees God in all people. It was sort of her way of making it through the world in a positive way.

I told her, "Too many people do horrible and heinous things to say that God is in all people. I might be able to come halfway to your statement and say God is *available* to all people, but he's sure not *in* all people." You only need a history book or even today's newspaper to see this is true. God and that kind of evil cannot exist in the same person at the same time.

PERVASIVE EVIL

Let's start with the bold claim that "God is in all people." I've got a few names that make me say: nope.

Foday Sankoh is one. He was the founder of the Revolutionary United Front in Sierra Leone, West Africa. His people were organized to use machetes and widespread rape to terrorize civilians of all ages and spread terror so they might take power. People still walk around in Sierra Leone with arms, feet, lips, or ears missing because of Sankoh. I don't think there was any of God in this man. Not even a little.

How about Ho Chi Minh? This man imprisoned and executed more than a quarter million of his own people. I don't think God was in Ho, nor does anyone else. Then there is Joseph Stalin. He used concentration camps and mass executions extensively, with a death toll in the tens of millions on his account. I think Stalin had something inside him other than God. How about Adolf Hitler? His atrocities are more well known, but all you need to do is study a little deeper to unveil the kind of evil that was not only in him, but in thousands of others who pursued the Holocaust and other atrocities of his era. I don't think he had "a little God in him," but he had a whole lot of evil in him.

I know it's not a popular idea, but I think we need to be up front with the reality that these things, and these people, are *evil*; in fact, there is a place for evil and it is not with God. It's definitely not Heaven—it's the opposite.

The God of the Bible is real, which makes Heaven for real, but it also makes hell for real. Why? Because of Sankoh and Ho and Hitler and Stalin. The blood of those they killed cries out for justice. But justice so often doesn't come in this life. The scales are not balanced. Punishment for evil is needed in the next life, especially when it doesn't come in this one. Jesus not only taught about Heaven, but also taught about hell, even more than he taught on Heaven.

This is the reason the Bible talks about Jesus being the judge of history. There will be a time when the scales of justice are re-balanced, and that involves judgment. It is not our role to judge other people, but you can be sure that it is the role of our God. It might not be our place to judge, but it is his place. Why? Evils need to be addressed. Judgment is needed.

HUMANISM ON THE ROPES

I can see why that publicist would adopt the idea that God is in all people, or at least that *good* is in all people. It's a very positive and uplifting message if you don't examine it too deeply.

It's a world full of hope and rainbows, and who doesn't want that? The problem is that it doesn't match reality. Don't you need an honest God, one who's not going to sugarcoat reality for you? Evil exists. Death and decay are all around us.

The philosophy the woman held is sometimes called humanism. I don't have some big beef against humanists, and I'm not going to throw them under the bus. I think their intent is good. They are trying to make the world a better place in the absence of believing in God. I get that. I just want to point out that the philosophy doesn't work; it doesn't explain the world, nor does it offer true hope for change.

The best example for this is that so much is getting worse, not better, when it is run by humans. With humanism, there is a belief that there is good in people, and they are capable of so much good if they work together. There is a slight tinge of hopefulness for a utopian society in it. That's not the humanist doctrine, but that's what it often leads to by implication.

Many have hoped for technology, democracy, and a spirit of human advancement to bring us to a utopian society where people are safe and selfless. Some think that if you just remove things like poverty and disease, then you will remove motivations for evil actions. But the advancements we've made have not made a dent in the human proclivity to evil. Utopia is nothing but a dream fully unattainable by human ingenuity and character.

The proof? That's where you need your newspaper and your history books. The ten most brutal genocides and wars in human history alone have totaled 250,259,749 deaths. Several were in the last few hundred years. Wars and terror are a part of the human experience. Left to our own, we murder and kill and bomb each other to oblivion.

Some might claim that things are getting better, but they aren't. The bloodiest war of all time was in the past century, World War II. Twelve of the worst genocides in human history occurred in the last century. Humanity is not getting better at this. We are getting worse. If humanism is to reflect reality, then it is a very dark road we are on.

Into this darkness comes the light, the light that gives life to humans: Jesus Christ. He became human so we might be saved from this fate. It is only through his grace that it is possible to fix any of our evil history.

SIN SEPARATES

The Bible makes it clear that God does not enjoy or set out to see people punished. God wants to save us. But sin grows and leads to more and more rebellion. And just as rebellion builds walls between people, it builds a wall between God and us. When we do evil—when we harbor sin in the docks of our hearts—that is the separating thing. It's not that God doesn't want to be with us, it's that we choose the sin over him. Isaiah 59:2 says it this way:

> It's your sins that have cut you off from God.
> Because of your sins, he has turned away
> and will not listen anymore.[1]

A familiar part of Scripture is John 3, where the great "God so loved the world that he gave his one and only son"[2] verse is found. Few go past verse 16, however, and read verses 17 through 21, which lay out the matters of judgment, punishment, and evil in the context of God's loving gift of his son for salvation. Understand that God loves, but God also must bring justice to bear for evil:

> God sent his Son into the world not to judge the world, but to save the world through him. There is no judgment against anyone who believes in him. But anyone who does not believe in him has already been judged for not believing in God's one and only Son. And the judgment is based on this fact: God's light came into the world, but people loved the darkness more than the light, for their actions were evil. All who do evil hate the light and refuse to go near it for fear their sins will be exposed. But those who do what is right come to the light so others can see that they are doing what God wants. (John 3:17–21 NLT)

In the end, those who do not want to be in the light choose to be in the darkness. This is true for Adolf Hitler, and even for those who are not guilty of genocide but instead choose what seem like minor evils. Even they are still choosing not to respond to the grace of God.

STUCK IN AN EVIL WORLD

I've loved reading Max Lucado's book *Because of Bethlehem*. Sure, it's a book about Christmas, but it's much more. He's helping us understand how Christmas is the celebration of the most important turning point in history for an evil world. In this book, Lucado helped me understand that all of us as human beings feel...stuck. We feel stuck in a dying body, stuck in bad habits, and stuck suffering the consequences of poor choices in our rebellious world. We need help. He says it this way: "...we shop till we drop, drink till we can't think, work till we can't stop. We do anything possible to get our minds off our mess, only to wake up, sober up, or sit up and realize we are all stuck. We need someone to save us from the meaninglessness and meanness...We need a Savior."[3]

The meanness is the evil of this world I'm speaking about. The reality is that human beings need something more than believing in other human beings to make things better. If all we have to go on is each other, then we're in trouble. Often what comes after this realization when you don't believe in God is the meaninglessness.

The publicist felt like there was a little God in all people. I would counter and say that there is a little evil in all people, and when we respond to God's free gift of salvation, we don't just get a "little God" in us. We don't just become "a little good." God takes in all of us, so that all of who we are submits to all of who he is.

Everything I was saying to the publicist was new information for her—a confrontation to the philosophy that there was a little God in all people. After hearing me express these kinds of ideas to her, the publicist began to reevaluate her position that God is in all people. She came to me the following day and told me she was struck by my comment about Hitler not having any good in him. It turned out she had a relative who had been in a Nazi concentration camp. She said to me, "When I was talking to you, there was a voice inside me telling me I needed to listen to you. I've never had that before. What was that?"

I was reminded of the verse that says, "Look! I stand at the door and knock. If you hear my voice and open the door, I will come in, and we will share a meal together as friends."[4] This is what was happening for this woman. This made her question easy to answer. "I'm praying for you and asking God to speak to you," I said. "So, the question is not *What is that?* It's *Who is that?* I believe God is already speaking to you."

Perhaps God is speaking to you as well. Maybe God is saying, "You need to listen to this." If so, then take the time to open that door and share some time with God, together as new friends.

21

NEXT STEPS

What should I do now? What's next for me?

A close buddy of mine frequently uses this phrase: "He's all hat and no cowboy." This is a western guy's way of saying: "He's all talk and no walk."

The reality is, we who follow Jesus can sometimes be all hat and no cowboy about our faith. We talk about this Jesus who changes lives, but our lives aren't changed. If we were firemen, we'd be all helmet and no firefighter. If we were priests, we'd be all collar and no soul. If we were football players, we'd be all uniform and no tackling.

It's time for our walk to match our talk.

How do we get there? Jesus works in each of us to grow proof in our lives that we are surrendered to him. Step one for everyone is to surrender your life to Christ—to be truly devoted to him. But what's step two? I know step one as sure as I know my own face, but I don't know your step two. You're going to have to let Jesus guide you through Scripture on what you need to do next.

THE COMMANDS OF JESUS

I don't know about you, but I just like to get to the point. I'd rather not mess around talking about nothing if we have business to get done or a decision to make. I'd rather get the elephant in the room on the table and carve that thing up into elephant steaks together, even if it's an awkward thing or a conflict.

If you're at all like that, then you may be wondering: What does Jesus want from me? You might be looking for a verse that gives you the marching orders for what's next. If there's a secret formula or recipe for how to live the Christian life, then you'd rather just know it now instead of being surprised with it later, even if it's difficult.

To answer these questions, we must look at what God says, so bear with me as we think through what God commanded of us. The short answer is: God gave us a lot of commands.

Don't be overwhelmed with despair. Think of all the things a child has to learn as he or she grows into life. Walking is only one of the difficult assignments; we won't even bring up language or relationships. Like a child learning to walk, there will be falls. There will stairs to master as well. There will be times when progress is slow and unsteady.

Gradually, growth and mastery will lead to speed and balance. All of these same steps occur when achieving spiritual growth as well. Rather than be afraid, decide to take another step. God smiles at your spiritual steps just as you applaud a child's physical ones.

What if you envisioned God's commands as steps? Steps can take you up a stairway that brings you closer to him. Steps can also take you higher in your relationship to others as each step takes your character higher, too.

Many think of the Old Testament as a bunch of rules and think of the New Testament as something without rules and commands. But if you do the math, it doesn't add up. The Jewish "Law" (known as the Torah) includes 613 commands the Jews sought to follow. In fact, if you've ever seen a devout Jew today wearing a prayer shawl (called the tallit), it is connected to these commands in the tassels. Each tassel has eight threads when doubled, and five sets of knots, making for thirteen. Added all up it makes 613 (or so they say . . . I for one have never counted the tassels).

That's a whole bunch of commands, but it is surprising to discover that there are more commands in the New Testament than in the entire Torah. Nearly seven hundred passages in the New Testament can be taken as commands. Jesus himself gave more than a hundred commands to his disciples and others wanting the same answer we're looking for.

Reading the dozens of commands from Jesus can be overwhelming. You risk getting to the point that you feel like you cannot please Jesus. But here's the thing: Jesus knows you, and knows what *you* need to do. Just like the rich young ruler we talked about earlier, Jesus knows which command you need to engage in to move to the next season of your spiritual life. For the rich young ruler, it was to lose his attachment to his possessions. But if you're not anything like him, it's likely something different for you. Maybe you're the Poor Old Everyman and not a rich young ruler. Well, then I'm guessing Jesus isn't telling you to go and sell everything you have and give it to the poor.

What follows is a whole long list of what Jesus told us to do. I'm not saying any of these are optional; perhaps over a lifetime Jesus would whisper into your soul and convict you on all these things. I'm just saying that if Jesus showed up in the place you are right now and told you to do just one thing next, it would likely be along the lines of one of these.

Here's the thing: The idea of Jesus being in the room with you right now is not hypothetical. I'm not saying this just to get you to think. The Spirit of God speaks for Jesus to you, and he can lay on your heart what you need to do next. Let's go through as many of these commands as possible in the first few chapters of the New Testament, in the book of Matthew. This is one of the most practical and simple portions of all Scripture. If you find yourself wondering, *Maybe this is the one for me next*, then pray about it and take the next step.[1]

IS JESUS TELLING YOU TO REPENT?

If you've never truly turned away from the sins that bring you down, then it's time. Jesus is asking you to repent, meaning turn from your sin. "From then on Jesus began to preach, 'Repent of your sins and turn to God, for the Kingdom of Heaven is near'" (Matthew 4:17). The next step is to take a full 180-degree turn away from sin and toward Jesus in full devotion.

IS JESUS TELLING YOU TO FOLLOW HIM?

If you've not decided to follow Jesus for the rest of your life, today is the day. This isn't a decision to become religious or be a Churchian—it is a decision to do what Jesus does and leave your life of apathy to call others to follow him, too. "Jesus called out to them, 'Come, follow me, and I will show you how to fish for people!'" (Matthew 4:19). The next step is to make a commitment, from this day through the end of your life, to follow him.

IS JESUS TELLING YOU TO REJOICE IN PERSECUTION?

Are you in hard times because of your new faith? Are people doing things to you to get you to give up your faith? If so, God has a strange view of that persecution: It makes you stronger in your faith and it's something to celebrate. "God blesses you when people mock you and persecute you and lie about you and say all sorts of evil things against you because you are my followers. Be happy about it! Be very glad! For a great reward awaits you in heaven. And remember, the ancient prophets were persecuted in the same way" (Matthew 5:11–12). The next step is to thank God for giving you the strength to withstand the persecution and for trusting you with it.

IS JESUS TELLING YOU TO GO PUBLIC?

Is your faith something you've only made private, and you need to go public with it? Do you need to demonstrate your love for those you know in a way that is unmistakably different? Are there those in your life who need to know why you've changed? "In the same way, let your good deeds shine out for all to see, so that everyone will praise your heavenly Father" (Matthew 5:16). The next step is to find a way to give God the glory for all he is doing in and through you.

IS JESUS TELLING YOU TO FORGIVE?

Is a grudge holding you back? Is there someone that you hold something against, or who holds something against you? If so, it is time to put that to rest, and even leave behind any other spiritual activity you are engaged in to make that right. "So if you are presenting a sacrifice at the altar in the Temple and you suddenly remember that someone has something against you, leave your sacrifice there at the altar. Go and be reconciled to that person. Then come and offer your sacrifice to God" (Matthew 5:23–24). The next step is to make a list of those you need to reconcile with, and do what it takes to love them and forgive them without trying to get them to admit any wrong.

IS JESUS TELLING YOU TO NOT LUST?

Are you harboring lustful thoughts in your mind instead of letting them go immediately? Do you dwell on the way someone looks, and desire them in a way that is corrupting your soul? "But I say, anyone who even looks at a woman with lust has already committed adultery with her in his heart" (Matthew 5:28). The next step is to let each lustful temptation go as soon as you think of it.

IS JESUS TELLING YOU TO KEEP YOUR WORD?

Do you have a problem with white lies? Are you even starting to believe some of your own made-up stories? It's time to be clear about the truth. "Just say a simple, 'Yes, I will,' or 'No, I won't.' Anything beyond this is from the evil one" (Matthew 5:37). The next step is to be ruthless with yourself to always tell the truth, and don't make promises you won't deliver on.

IS JESUS TELLING YOU TO PRAY IN SECRET?

Do you tend to seek praise and look for credit from others, even in spiritual things? Do you do one thing in front of others, and another in private? It's time to make your spiritual life more secret. "When you pray, don't be like the hypocrites who love to pray publicly on street corners and in the synagogues where everyone can see them. I tell you the truth, that is all the reward they will ever get. But when you pray, go away by yourself, shut the door behind you, and pray to your Father in private. Then your Father, who sees everything, will reward you" (Matthew 6:5–6). The next step is to develop spiritual practices that are completely secret, and that no one else will ever know about but you and God.

IS JESUS TELLING YOU TO INVEST IN HEAVEN?

Do you only invest in things that don't last? Is God asking you to invest in his Kingdom where it counts—with your wallet? If you are slow to give up your finances to God, he may be asking you to surrender this part of your value system to him. "Don't store up treasures here on earth, where moths eat them and rust destroys them, and where thieves break in and steal. Store your treasures in heaven, where moths and rust cannot destroy, and thieves do not break in and steal. Wherever your treasure is, there the desires of your heart will also be" (Matthew 6:19–21). The next step is to find a way to give to make God's work move forward, without any consideration for getting credit or gain for yourself, but rather out of the generosity of your heart. This will change you forever.

IS JESUS TELLING YOU TO SEEK HIS KINGDOM?

Do you wake up in the morning and go to bed at night obsessed with something other than godly thoughts? Is there some goal in your life that has not been submitted to God's plan? Perhaps God is asking you to put that thing into his hands, and seek his way to attain it, if at all, if he is not first. "Seek the Kingdom of God above all else, and live righteously, and he will give you everything you need" (Matthew 6:33). The next step is to consider how your goals fit into God's plan, and to either align them with him, or abandon them altogether.

IS JESUS TELLING YOU TO NOT JUDGE?

Do you tend to look down on others for this or that quality, or for some behavior? Are you thinking too often about the negative qualities of others that annoy you or offend you? God may be asking you to leave that judgment up to him so your thoughts may become more positive. "Do not judge others, and you will not be judged. For you will be treated as you treat others. The standard you use in judging is the standard by which you will be judged. And why worry about a speck in your friend's eye when you have a log in your own?" (Matthew 7:1–3). The next step is to trust God to handle these people that you want to judge, and live your life with more positive focus.

IS JESUS TELLING YOU TO STOP WASTING YOUR EFFORTS?

Are you putting a great deal of effort into pleasing people who cannot be pleased? Are you trying to do something that honors people instead of God? Perhaps God wants to release you from feeling like you're banging your head against the wall. "Don't waste what is holy on people who are unholy. Don't throw your pearls to pigs! They will trample the pearls, then turn and attack you" (Matthew 7:6). The next step is to give your obsession with this over to God, and to find a way to not only trust him, but work to please him instead.

IS JESUS TELLING YOU TO ASK HIM FOR WHAT YOU NEED?

Is your pride keeping you from dependence on God? Do you have needs you aren't willing to admit to, because that would be a sign of weakness? God may want you to be persistent in bringing your need to him. "Keep on asking, and you will receive what you ask for. Keep on seeking, and you will find. Keep on knocking, and the door will be opened to you. For everyone who asks, receives. Everyone who seeks, finds. And to everyone who knocks, the door will be opened" (Matthew 7:7–8). The next step is to understand that God truly wants the best for you and will provide what you truly need, and redirect your desires to more noble things if you truly do not.

IS JESUS TELLING YOU TO TREAT OTHERS DIFFERENTLY?

Are you treating people in a way that may not be the best? Do you expect a certain level of service from others, but then you do not serve others in your home, or your work, or your community? God may be asking you to become a servant like him. "Do to others whatever you would like them to do to you. This is the essence of all that is taught in the law and the prophets" (Matthew 7:12). The next step is to make this command, often called the Golden Rule, a part of how you treat other people, selflessly.

IS JESUS TELLING YOU TO CHOOSE THE HARD PATH?

Is it your tendency to do things the easy way and take the shortcut? Do you need to be tested by God and do something difficult for him in your life? Perhaps God wants to see what you're made of, and is calling you to a hard path next. "You can enter God's Kingdom only through the narrow gate. The highway to hell is broad, and its gate is wide for the many who choose that way. But the gateway to life is very narrow and the road is difficult, and only a few ever find it" (Matthew 7:13–14). The next step is to choose the hard thing God wants from you, to take your dedication to another level and take the narrow path others wouldn't take, because God believes you can do it by his power.

IS JESUS TELLING YOU TO BE MORE DISCERNING?

Do you trust someone more than you should who is in a position of authority, but is misusing that power? Have you become enamored with a person over Jesus Christ, and are no longer discerning the leaders from one another? If you are following someone more closely than you are following Jesus, then redirect to follow him. "Beware of false prophets who come disguised as harmless sheep but are really vicious wolves. You can identify them by their fruit, that is, by the way they act. Can you pick grapes from thornbushes, or figs from thistles?" (Matthew 7:15–16). The next step is to get godly wisdom from others, to pray and examine Scripture, and discern if the person you are following is causing you to show more of the fruit God wants in your life.

NO FORMULAS

After a large event where God had moved in a great way, we were going through the prayer and response cards. One card stood out to me more than any other. It was from a woman who noted by checking a box that she understood the message of Jesus we presented and had surrendered her life to Christ for the first time at the event. We celebrated that!

But there is more to the story. Thousands have responded to Christ at our events, but this one had a few other things going on. She also noted on her card that her partner needed prayer; her partner was another grandmother who had been denied access to her grandchild. She followed that with excitement about what God was doing in her heart that night, and concluded with this exclamation: "Let's go kick Satan's *** together!"

There's a lot going on here on this little card. *What should I be praying for, for this woman*, I thought.

Should I be praying for a next step in the vulgar language she uses (even on a prayer card)?

Should I be praying for next steps about the fact that she's all gung-ho to fight Satan "out there" with us but there's a lot inside her that needs God's wholeness?

Should I be praying for next steps for the relationship she is in?

Should I pray for next steps with the estranged grandchild and the longing for being reconnected?

This was hard to discern. But of course, the truth quickly became apparent from Christ to me. The key was that she had responded to Jesus that night, and she'd invited him in. That was the most important next step for her. What was God going to do in and through her next? I don't know. I just know that my role in her life that night was to introduce her to Jesus and his message, which she received.

Our role with others is to love them, pray for them, present the truth of Jesus, and then come alongside them over time to help them discern what God is leading them to do in their lives next according to the Bible.

You see, for each of us it's not about focusing on all the steps at once. It's about the *next* steps. Well-meaning people make a mistake when establishing a formula for others in their spiritual lives. I'm not going to do that for you. God, not me, must speak to you. Jesus is always step one in any spiritual growth, we know that—but we can't formulate the next steps for others beyond that. People need God, not our formula. It's crucial to be patient and let God be God, and obey him when he speaks.

22

LAST WORDS

What are you trying to say to me?

In writing this book, I've been thinking of two kinds of people. The first is the non-church-person, the one who
believes just a little bit but wouldn't consider him- or herself a
churchgoing religious person. The Bible has a word for that
kind of person. I hope it doesn't offend you. It's the word *rebellious*.

Now, you may be the kind that embraces the idea of being a
rebel, a modern-day James Dean. Regardless of your perspective, we are all rebels against God when we are born, and my
hope with this book has been to speak to people who have been
rebels. I can relate; I have a bit of a rebel spirit in me, too.
The Scripture that has guided my calling of late has been Luke
1:17b: "He will cause those who are rebellious to accept the
wisdom of the godly."[1]

So, how do I define *rebellious*? Well, we all struggle with
guilt. The problem with recognizing morality is that we begin

to feel guilt. It keeps us apart from God. With guilt, we either draw closer to God and receive forgiveness, or we keep God at a distance, so that we think of God less and think about our guilt less. All of us are naturally rebellious. It is the "teenager spirit" I've mentioned. I want all of us with a teenager spirit to accept the wisdom of the godly.

Of course, you may find it hard to accept the *wisdom of the godly*, so let's talk about that. I understand why you might feel that way. I am here to ask your forgiveness for the way so many of the supposedly godly have misrepresented the message of Jesus—those I've called the Churchians in this book (as opposed to true Christians). Churchians among us have done you a disservice. Please forgive us, and don't hold our behavior against God.

That verse I just quoted, in Luke 1, came to Zechariah and Elizabeth, who were unable to have a child. I don't know if you've ever felt literally or figuratively barren like Elizabeth, as if nothing you were doing was producing what you intended. I believe that God can work miracles again as he did for her when he gave her a son. I am praying for a new day for you. You are barren no more; you're going to be fruitful from here on out. God can give you the love, joy, and peace that you are looking for. Perhaps your heart or your family or your work or your life feels empty and barren like Elizabeth's womb. I'm here to tell you about the wisdom of the godly, that God can help give to you what has been missing when you feel barren. Start your new day now.

The other people I have had in mind in this book are Christian people. I am concerned that I must apologize for the church as I did in the previous paragraphs. Following Jesus Christ has been so watered down that repentance (true change) has often been discarded. Many have disposed of the inconvenient message of repentance the way you would throw trash in a dumpster.

In the Bible, forgiveness is never offered without repentance. Grace is undeserved, but it's never cheap. Pastors offer it like a couple of ounces of cocoa in your milk, something they dispense to sweeten up your life. Salvation is much more costly and real than that.

My message to Christians is to repent of the godless churchy fakery we are tempted to entertain in both our lives and our churches. And instead seek real repentance, true life change.

The Apostle Paul talked about why it is so important to make this message about forgiveness clear: "I am not sorry that I sent that severe letter to you, though I was sorry at first, for I know it was painful to you for a little while. Now I am glad I sent it, not because it hurt you, but because the pain caused you to repent and change your ways. It was the kind of sorrow God wants his people to have, so you were not harmed by us in any way. For the kind of sorrow God wants us to experience leads us away from sin and results in salvation. There's no regret for that kind of sorrow. But worldly sorrow, which lacks repentance, results in spiritual death."[2]

MY STORY

Jesus headed to a village called Nain, and a large crowd followed him. A funeral procession was coming out of the village as he approached. Today we don't have the same kind of experience, but we do have the procession of cars leaving a funeral to go to the burial. The hearse comes, then the car with the family, then a bunch of cars with their lights on, even at midday, and many have little flags on them. I don't know what they do in your town, but in mine we all pull our cars over to the side of the road for a moment and let the procession pass. It's a solemn moment, even if you have no idea who the deceased is. I experience these moments from the distance of my car, however. Behind the safety and obscurity of tinted windows, I cannot see or hear those who are crying. This wasn't true in the time of Jesus. Then they stood in the open. They saw and heard the pain, especially the mother's.

Jesus considered the eyes of every mourner. The Bible says, "The young man who had died was a widow's only son, and a large crowd from the village was with her. When the Lord saw her, his heart overflowed with compassion." Then he said something not one of us would ever think to say. "'Don't cry!' he said. Then he walked over to the coffin and touched it, and the bearers stopped. 'Young man,' he said, 'I tell you, get up.' Then the dead boy sat up and began to talk! And Jesus gave him back to his mother."[3]

I don't know what this boy could have said to his mom. I don't know anything about the ensuing conversations. But just like you, I compare other people's lives with my own experiences. I can only imagine what conversations occurred. Were their talks as intense or as life changing as mine were with Colton? By now you have to recognize that this story is so similar to my own. I know both the fear of the mother in losing a child, and then the joy when that child is given back. My son told me, in no uncertain terms, that Jesus sent him back from Heaven because he was answering my prayer. I know that just as Jesus gave this child back to his mother, he also gave my son back to me.

This story has become my story. Since 2003, I've had the chance to talk about this unexplainable but undeniable miracle God has done in my life. I know that same unexplainable, undeniable God wants to do amazing things in your life, too. In fact, I think every real Christ follower has their own story of some sort, a place where God met them. A moment when God confirmed his love for them. A spot in time when God wrapped his arms around them and said, "I'm here."

Knowing what God did for me, I've always wondered how I could repay him. Even though I try to talk and share about him, I know there is nothing I can do to pay him back. But that's the whole point. Jesus has done it. Jesus has already taken care of that for all of us. Just as he held my son on his lap, he longs to hold you in Heaven as well.

MY PRAYER FOR YOU

I am praying you'll recognize that your Creator God is for real, and that he made you for a purpose. I am praying that the realization—which I think you've already had—will grow in you to have the sense to respond to God. Believing in God and not having it change your life is senseless. I want your heart to fully turn to God. Because of this, I'm praying Psalm 119:73

for you: "You made me; you created me. Now give me the sense to follow your commands."[4]

I am praying that this book has helped you ponder the direction of your life, and that you're at the point of turning to truly follow God. I think right now is the time for you to say, "No turning back," whether you're new to the faith or you've believed before but just haven't been taking God seriously enough. Because of this I'm also praying Psalm 119:59 for you: "I pondered the direction of my life, and I turned to follow your laws."[5]

Are you ready for God to be more real than ever before in your life? Believe in him, because if there's anything I'm sure of, it's that God is for real.

I cry out to the LORD; I plead for the LORD's mercy.
I pour out my complaints before him and tell him all my troubles.
When I am overwhelmed, you alone know the way I should turn.
Wherever I go, my enemies have set traps for me.
I look for someone to come and help me, but no one gives me a passing thought!
No one will help me; no one cares a bit what happens to me.
Then I pray to you, O LORD. I say, "You are my place of refuge.
You are all I really want in life." (Psalm 142:1–5 NLT)

NOTES

CHAPTER 3 NOTES

1 John 1:5 NLT

CHAPTER 4 NOTES

1 Mark 10:19 NLT

CHAPTER 5 NOTES

1 Genesis 3:6 NLT
2 Genesis 3:7 NLT
3 1 Kings 19:9 NLT
4 Genesis 3:12 NIV
5 Mark 14:30 NLT

CHAPTER 6 NOTES

1 Matthew 23:13 NLT
2 Luke 13:15–16 NLT
3 Matthew 21:29–31 NLT
4 Matthew 21:23 NLT

5 Matthew 21:31–32 NLT
6 NLT
7 Acts 11:26 NLT
8 2 Peter 1:4 NLT
9 Jeremiah 29:11–12 NLT
10 Isaiah 46:4 NLT
11 Matthew 11:28 NLT

CHAPTER 7 NOTES

1 NIV
2 Jeremiah 29:13 NIV
3 Albert Bigelow Paine, *Mark Twain, A Biography: The Personal and Literary Life of Samuel Langhorne Clemens*, vols. 3 and 4 (New York: Harper & Brothers, 1912), 1,567.

CHAPTER 8 NOTES

1 Romans 6:6 NLT
2 Romans 6:12 NLT

CHAPTER 9 NOTES

1 NLT
2 Genesis 12:3 NIV
3 Genesis 22:18 NIV
4 Zechariah 8:13 NIV
5 See Isaiah 7:14, Micah 5:2, and Hosea 11:1
6 See Jeremiah 31:15, Isaiah 11:1, and Isaiah 9:1–2
7 See Psalm 41:9, Zechariah 11:12–13, and Psalm 22:7–8
8 See Psalm 22:16 and Zechariah 12:10
9 See Psalm 22:18

NOTES

10 Luke 1:30-33 NLT
11 Luke 24:13 NLT
12 Luke 24:17 NLT
13 Luke 24:19–24 NLT
14 See Isaiah 7:14, Micah 5:2, and Hosea 11:1
15 See Jeremiah 31:15, Isaiah 11:1, and Isaiah 9:1–2
16 See Psalm 41:9, Zechariah 11:12–13, and Psalm 22:7–8
17 See Psalm 22:16–18 and Zechariah 12:10
18 Luke 24:32 NLT

CHAPTER 10 NOTES

1 Matthew 7:9–11 NIV
2 John 14:1–2 NIV
3 Proverbs 3:5 NIV
4 Philippians 4:7 NIV

CHAPTER 11 NOTES

1 Luke 23:41–42 NLT
2 Luke 23:43 NLT
3 Psalm 90:8 NLT
4 Hebrews 12:1–2 NIV

CHAPTER 12 NOTES

1 Story used with permission.
2 Luke 6:43 NIV
3 As quoted in Nancie Carmichael, *Praying for Rain: Surrender & Triumph in Life's Desert Experiences* (Nashville: Thomas Nelson, 2001).
4 Hebrews 10:24 NIV

CHAPTER 13 NOTES

1 The story of Jesus and Caesar's tax is in Matthew 22:15–22. Quotes used here are from the NIV version.
2 Jeremiah 29:7 NIV
3 2 Chronicles 20:12 NIV
4 Daniel 1–2
5 Matthew 6:10 ESV
6 Colossians 1:13 NLT

CHAPTER 14 NOTES

1 Joshua 2:15
2 Joshua 3:15
3 Accessed on March 18, 2017, from http://creation.com/the-walls-of-jericho#r4
4 Joshua 2:11b NIV
5 Joshua 2:10 NIV
6 Joshua 2:9b, 2:11a NIV
7 Joshua 2:9a NIV

CHAPTER 15 NOTES

1 Accessed on March 13, 2017, from https://www.youtube.com/watch?v=v0_2hLKuCBU
2 Revelation 12:11 NLT
3 2 Corinthians 12:9a NLT
4 Accessed on March 18, 2017, from http://www.gutenberg.org/files/18269/18269-h/18269-h.htm
5 John 9:25 NIV
6 List quoted and adapted from David Drury, *Transforming Presence: How Being with Jesus Changes Everything* (Wesleyan Publishing

NOTES

CHAPTER 16 NOTES

1 1 Peter 3:15b NIV
2 Philippians 1:7b NIV
3 Titus 1:9 NIV

CHAPTER 17 NOTES

1 Accessed on March 13, 2017, from http://www.vanityfair.com/news/2015/12/martin-shkreli-pharmaceuticals-ceo-interview
2 Accessed on March 13, 2017, from http://time.com/4510707/martin-shkreli-auction-face-punch
3 Accessed on March 13, 2017, from http://www.vanityfair.com/news/2015/12/martin-shkreli-pharmaceuticals-ceo-interview
4 Revelation 21:5a NLT
5 See The Issachar Project.

CHAPTER 18 NOTES

1 Romans 8:28 NIV
2 Kurt Vonnegut, *Bagombo Snuff Box: Uncollected Short Fiction* (New York: G. P. Putnam's Sons, 1999), 9–10.

CHAPTER 19 NOTES

1 John 16:33 NIV
2 Revelation 21:3–5 NLT
3 1 John 4:4 NIV
4 NAS
5 Job 4:17–21 NLT

6 Job 4:12 NLT
7 Job 4:13–18 NLT
8 "I will obey your decrees. Please don't give up on me!"—Psalm
   119:8 NLT
9 James 1:16–17a NLT
10 Matthew 5:45 NLT

CHAPTER 20 NOTES

1 NLT
2 NIV
3 Max Lucado, *Because of Bethlehem* (Nashville: Thomas Nelson,
   2016), 123.
4 Revelation 3:20 NLT

CHAPTER 21 NOTES

1 All passages used in this chapter are from the NLT.

CHAPTER 22 NOTES

1 NLT
2 2 Corinthians 7:8–10 NLT
3 Luke 7:12–15 NLT
4 NLT
5 NLT

ABOUT THE AUTHORS

Todd Burpo is the pastor of Crossroads Wesleyan Church in Imperial, Nebraska. He was ordained in 1994. He is the best-selling author of *Heaven Is for Real, Heaven Is for Real for Kids,* and *Heaven Is for Real for Little Ones.* He is also the coauthor, along with his wife, Sonja, of *Heaven Changes Everything.* Todd can be found working shoulder-to-shoulder with the Imperial Volunteer Fire Department as a firefighter. He is also the chaplain for the Nebraska State Volunteer Firefighters Association. Todd has operated an overhead door company, coached wrestling, and served on the local school board.

David Drury is the author or coauthor of nine books, including *Transforming Presence, Being Dad,* and *SoulShift.* David has been chief of staff for the Wesleyan Church headquarters since 2012, and can be found online at DavidDrury.com.